GREGOR n for the outdoors with his love of Scottish history in undertaking the six-week journey that led to *Charlie, Meg and Me*. Always looking to widen his knowledge of Scotland's past, he is as happy trawling through a tome by a warm fire as he is exploring ruins and battlefields. His outdoor exploits were initially a means of gaining fitness, but after completing the Duke of Edinburgh Award and steadily ticking off Munros, he has come to appreciate the beauty and freedom of Scotland's remote landscapes more than ever. Gregor is based in Falkirk, where he works in property management and lives with his wife, Nicola, their three daughters, Sophie, Kara and Abbie, and their dogs, Meg and Ailsa.

I suspect this will rapidly become the companion volume of choice for the growing number of walkers setting out to follow in George Ewing's footsteps.
NORTHWARDS NOW

… a celebration of self-sufficiency and living in harmony with nature.
SCOTTISH FIELD

Charlie, Meg and Me

An epic 530 mile walk recreating
Bonnie Prince Charlie's escape after
the disaster of Culloden

GREGOR EWING

Luath Press Limited
EDINBURGH
www.luath.co.uk

First Published 2013
Reprinted 2013

ISBN: 978-1-908373-61-8

The paper used in this book is recyclable. It is made
from low chlorine pulps produced in a low energy,
low emissions manner from renewable forests.

Printed and bound by
Charlesworth Press, Wakefield

Typeset in 10 point Sabon
by 3btype.com

Maps © Gregor Ewing. Base map information supplied
by Open Street & Cycle Map (and) contributors
(www.openstreetmap.org), and reproduced under the
Creative Commons Licence.

Images on page 14 and 231, and on page 1 of colour section are
reproduced under the Creative Commons Licence.

Contents

List of Maps   6

Acknowledgements   8

Foreword by Dr Tony Pollard   9

Notes on the text   12

Prologue   13

CHAPTER 1   Introduction   19

CHAPTER 2   From Culloden to Arisaig   28

CHAPTER 3   The Western Isles   64

CHAPTER 4   The Isles of Skye and Raasay   104

CHAPTER 5   Mallaig to Glen Shiel   127

CHAPTER 6   Glen Cannich then Lochiel country   161

CHAPTER 7   To Badenoch   188

CHAPTER 8   Loch nan Uamh   210

Epilogue   232

Timeline   234

Bibliography   237

List of Maps

The Complete Journey 7

From Drummossie Moor to Loch Lochy 27

Towards Arisaig 51

Lewis and Harris 63

Benbecula and South Uist 79

Northern Skye and Raasay 103

Sligachan to Elgol 119

Knoydart to MacEachen's Refuge 126

Crossing the Rough Bounds 142

To Glen Cannich then southwards 160

Loch Garry to Achnacarry 179

Towards Fort Augustus 187

To Badenoch 196

From the Cage to Glen Roy 209

Towards the West Coast 215

To Loch nan Uamh 223

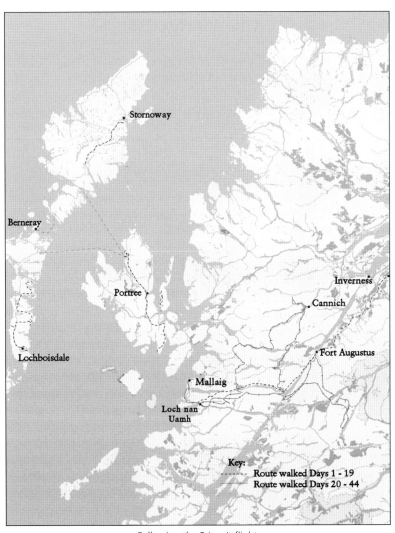

Following the Prince's flight

Acknowledgements

MY JOURNEY WOULD not have happened without the support and encouragement of Nicola, my wife. This book is dedicated to her and also to my children Sophie, Kara and Abbie who mean the world to me.

I owe a big debt of gratitude to the support team who helped keep the home fires burning whilst I was away: Diane, Janet, Susan, Carol, Gordon, Emma-Louise, Mum and Dad.

Thanks to Gavin MacDougall for his encouragement. The knowledge that Luath Press were behind me helped from day one of the trip.

I really appreciated all the friendship, support and help that I was given on my journey. Not least from my old friend George, my new friend Alistair MacEachen and from Deirdre MacEachen, Bob Forgie, Sarah at Arisaig House and Lyn at Raasay House Outdoor Centre,

Finally a special thanks to Kate Fawcett, Ian Scott and Kirsten Graham who proof read the manuscript, sorted out my grammar, spelling, inaccuracies and provided helpful suggestions.

Foreword

THERE IS NO better way to appreciate history than to visit the places touched by it. I constantly impress this point on my students, most particularly when studying battlefields – if you are to have any chance of understanding what happened at Flodden, Culloden or Waterloo you really need to visit the ground, walk it and appreciate the terrain – only then will you understand the decisions that commanders made and why events unfolded as they did. The same is true of any journey made by people in the past. While we cannot walk in someone else's shoes nor perhaps not even in their footsteps, we can get an idea of the challenges any arduous route throws up and the emotions which the landscape might elicit. Anyone who doesn't believe that only needs to read this book to be convinced otherwise.

Gregor is by no means the first person to be attracted to the epic journey taken by Charles Edward Stuart, better known as Bonnie Prince Charlie, during his time as a fugitive following defeat at the Battle of Culloden on 16 April 1746. I recall many years ago watching the TV series 'In the Footsteps of Bonnie Prince Charlie' with Jimmie MacGregor, and then there is the book 'Walking with Charlie' by Steve Lord, to name but two examples. Of course, Jimmie MacGregor didn't walk the whole route and although Steve Lord walked more of it, he negotiated it in sections, returning to the comfort of his home for long stretches before taking up the trail again. Gregor's journey was different – he did the whole thing in a single stint over a period of six weeks, and it's the first time that anyone has done that, apart from Charlie of course.

One of the strengths of this man and dog travelogue, which as such takes its place alongside John Steinbeck's aptly titled but totally unrelated 'Travels with Charley', is the neat way it stitches together history with the writer's personal journey. The balance is perfect and even a supposed expert like me comes away feeling I've learned something thanks to Gregor taking me back to 1746 when he reaches the relevant points on his walk.

The real star of the show however isn't Gregor, and not even his trusty sidekick, Meg the dog, it's the landscape of northwest Scotland and the isles. I spent the later part of my childhood in that part of the world and return to it whenever possible. I would challenge anyone to read this book and not by the end of it want to strap on their walking boots and get onto the hills and into the glens. But beauty comes with a price and the unforgiving nature of the place looms large here. It is in sharing Gregor's difficulties in coping with what, despite the roads and ferries, still comes across pretty much as a wilderness that we get a vivid idea of the straits in which the Prince found himself. It was a long walk from Culloden to the shores of Loch nan Uamh, from where the Prince was finally picked up by a French ship, and there were a lot of detours and encounters with people on the way, and the following pages do much to bring that journey without maps to life.

As an archaeologist I am perhaps most familiar with the starting point for that journey, having carried out various surveys and excavations of the battlefield at Culloden, and it was there, several years ago now, that I ended a journey into the past of my own. A friend and I had the bright idea of recreating another walk made by Bonnie Prince Charlie, the night march which the Jacobite army made in attempt to surprise the Duke of Cumberland in camp at Nairn on the night of 15–16 Arpil 1746. We decided to do it in period kit, carrying the weapons of the day and accompanied by a platoon of eager re-enactors. We set out from Culloden House, where Charles had set up his HQ, at around seven o'clock in the evening with a spring in our step and the press in tow. However, as the night drew on the fatigue set in. Swords and muskets, which at first seemed to weigh nothing, began to show their true colours. By the time we got within a couple of miles or so of Nairn, at around two in the morning, by which time I had already abandoned my sword and musket, we were all shattered and decided to a man to turn back, at a spot which can't have been that far away from where the Jacobite army decided to call it a night. So, we turned and headed back, this time for Culloden battlefield.

I arrived there at around five thirty in the morning to find just a couple of the others hanging around. Plans to have some sort of assembly at the clan monument were forgotten as weary men melted away back to their homes. It was at that point I realised I could barely move – my thighs and nether regions were in agony after wearing a kilt (full plaid) for over 20 miles. When I got back to my hotel – which shamed me as those who made the journey in 1746 then had to fight a battle – I could barely make it into the bath. Later that day I learned that less than half the party had made it back to Culloden without the aid of a support vehicle and one among us was in hospital after going over on his ankle in the dark.

There had been some talk of retracing the Jacobite march to Derby, a much more ambitious undertaking, but after that night it was never a conversation injected with much enthusiasm. The Nairn walk had however been a success, in that it had shown just how big a mistake that march in 1746 had been. The Jacobites would have been far better off getting what rest they could before the battle rather than wasting all that energy on what turned out to be wild goose chase. That experience also helped me appreciate just how big an accomplishment Gregor's epic 500 mile journey had been, and for that I take my blue bonnet off to him. There is a rumour that his next expedition will follow the advances made by the Marquis of Montrose in the mid 1600s. If it is then I hope the road rises up to meet him, and Meg of course.

Tony Pollard
Loch Fyne
February 2013

Notes on the text

Although I believe imperial measures give most people a better sense of perspective (thus my subtitle!) I had no option but to think metric during my journey because that's the way maps are made. I apologise to any imperial thinkers, but as a reminder:

1 kilometre = 0.6 Mile.

Everyone has their own method of working this out, but to get miles I half the kilometre distance and add 20 per cent.

Where Gaelic words are included in the text, landscape features are named as they appear on Ordnance Survey maps. A few of the more commonly repeated words are:

'Bealach'	Pass or a low point between two hills
'Allt'	Burn or stream.
'Coire'	Corrie, a hollow in the side of or between two hills.
'Sgurr'	Rocky or steep peak
'Beinn'	Mountain or peak
'Meall'	Rounded hill
'Sron'	Nose, point

Prologue

ON 23 JULY 1745, Charles Edward Stuart landed on the Isle of Eriskay in the Western Isles. With no money, arms or troops and only seven attendants he aimed to restore his father, James, to the unified throne of England, Scotland and Ireland. The Prince had not set out from France entirely empty handed, but a second accompanying ship carrying 700 troops, money and armaments was badly damaged in a skirmish with a British man-of-war en-route, and was forced to return to France.

Without French assistance, Highland chiefs who had previously pledged their support, now refused to rise, but, by the sheer force of his personality, Charles managed to convince them, one by one, to rally to his cause. In a key moment at Arisaig, Charles convinced Donald Cameron of Lochiel to raise his clan, support which was instrumental in helping the rising to gather momentum.

The standard was famously raised at Glenfinnan on 19 August 1745. Significant numbers of men were rallied; Lochiel provided 700 Camerons and MacDonald of Keppoch brought 300 of his clansmen. The government's response was to offer a £30,000 (approximately £1,000,000 in today's terms) reward for the capture of Charles.

The Jacobites travelled light and fast, moving south over the Corrieyairack Pass where a government army commanded by General Cope refused battle and retreated back to Inverness. The Highlanders formed an immediate bond with their Prince, who led from the front and marched with the men.

Thus, by early September with hardly a blow struck, the town of Perth was captured and occupied in the name of James VIII. Charles appointed Lord George Murray as Lieutenant General. Murray was a capable soldier, but the subsequent breakdown in the relationship between these two men was a key factor in how the campaign eventually played out.

Edinburgh was captured without bloodshed on 17 September. The Highlanders streamed into a gate left open by the deputation who had been parleying with Charles outside the city. The Prince was declared regent and housed himself in Holyrood Palace.

Bonnie Prince Charlie (1892) by John Pettie.
At Holyrood with young MacDonald of Clanranald on the left and
Cameron of Lochiel on the right.

On 21 September, the Jacobites won the Battle of Prestonpans, defeating General Cope's government troops in less than ten minutes. The only army in Scotland opposing the Jacobites was removed.

Charles established his reputation as the young chevalier: magnanimous, handsome, popular. On 10 October, he issued a declaration to revise the Act of Union between Scotland and England. (McLynn, F; *Bonnie Prince Charlie*; Pimlico, London; 2003)

A council of war was held to consider an invasion of England. A vote was taken and the decision to invade was made with a majority of only one vote. Charles wished to attack General Wade's army at Newcastle, but he eventually acceded to Lord George Murray's invasion plan, avoiding the confrontation with Wade's forces.

In November the Prince crossed into England at the head of 4,500 troops, and after a brief siege Carlisle was captured. The march south continued without any interference but, other than a regiment of 400 formed at Manchester, few rallied to the Prince's cause.

On 5 December, the army reached Derby having avoided any set battles and outmanoeuvring the opposition at every turn. The downside of this strategy was that there were now government forces to their flank as well as behind them. Furthermore, a Hanoverian spy informed the Jacobite council of war that a third government army was waiting at Northampton, ready to protect London.

The Jacobites were hindered by the lack of credible intelligence available to them. They were unaware that this third army was a fabrication. Neither did they realise that General Wade's army was still many miles behind them, nor that the Duke of Cumberland's army may not have been able to intercept the Jacobite army had it made a dash for London (Duffy, C; *The '45*; Cassell, London; 2003).

With no additional military aid arising, Charles' promises of a French invasion and, significant support from English or Welsh Jacobites had been laid bare. A council of war voted unanimously to retreat, much to the Prince's contempt.

The retreat began on 6 December, with Charles in a sour mood. English towns were much more hostile on the way north. A skirmish took place at Clifton, 12 days later, where Cumberland's Cavalry and Dragoon infantry were rebuffed. The Prince refused to release more troops preventing a possible full-scale victory.

On 26 December, the Jacobites entered Glasgow and Charles reviewed his army on Glasgow Green. The Prince found few active supporters in this town, which had gained prosperity since the Act of Union.

On 17 January, the Battle of Falkirk took place on the moors above the town. General Henry Hawley's forces were sent packing back towards Edinburgh. Charles wanted to follow up the victory by marching on the capital right away but Lord George Murray opposed this. With the support of the Clan Chiefs, Lord George wanted to retreat to the Highlands to re-launch the campaign in the spring, which Charles reluctantly accepted.

With Charles ill, leaving the command of his forces to Lord George Murray and others, the Jacobites achieved various small victories against the remaining government troops in Scotland. However, as Cumberland's army approached, the Jacobites failed to defend the River Spey, a key geographical barrier.

An audacious night attack on Cumberland's army was abandoned on 15 April. At 2am, Lord George calculated that the Jacobites would fail to reach the government encampment before first light and called off the attack. (Duffy, C; *The '45*; Cassell, London; 2003)

Etchings of Charles Edward Stuart and William The Duke of Cumberland.
Courtesy of Inverness Museum and Art Gallery

Despite the protests of Lord George Murray and others, Charles was determined to do battle at Culloden on 16 April. The tired, outnumbered Jacobites were drawn up on Drummossie Moor to await the Duke of Cumberland's army.

(Except where otherwise noted, based on dates and events contained in *Itinerary of Prince Charles Edward Stuart* by WB Blaikie and published by the Scottish History Society in 1897.)

CHAPTER I

Introduction

I HAVE HAD A long felt desire to escape to Scotland's hills. To spend weeks amongst stunning scenery that stirs the blood, high mountains, wide valleys and hidden glens. Enjoying unbounded freedom and tranquillity in an unspoiled landscape. Being in tune with oneself, melding with the natural environment; reaching a mountaintop with stunning views in all directions; wild camping beside an overshadowed lochan or on a small plateau beside a mountain stream; enjoying the primitive calmness of sitting, well fed, around a campfire; the fulfilment of resting with a light-headed tiredness that comes after a day's exertion; being totally responsible for oneself and buzzing from the increased confidence that self-sufficiency brings. All this may sound a little naïve: you can be soaked through to the skin in no time and walking in mist all day. The novelty of camping can soon wear off. Injuries can happen. Crucial equipment can be forgotten, broken or left out in the rain. Midges can drive you to murder/suicide/another continent. Countless things can go wrong. But even after years of experiencing what Scotland's outdoors can throw at you, the desire still burned bright.

For a long time, such a journey was simply a pipe dream. I had a busy job, and a young family. Could the desire be simply a reaction to an increasingly difficult career and the responsibility of family life? Where was that free time I enjoyed when young and single? And what had I done *with* that free time? Sadly, precious little. Now when I wasn't helping around the house, entertaining the kids or working extra hours, I really appreciated time alone. The occasional weekend was the best I could muster. Climb a few hills, stay out overnight, climb a few more hills and home. Great fun? Yes! But it still didn't placate my desire, I needed something more. I wanted my escape to be a sufficient length of time to shake off the modern world. A chance to draw breath and take stock, allowing reflection to happen at a natural pace. Tuning in to my surroundings and allowing the mind to relax, whilst pushing myself physically to see if I could survive for a sustained period of time.

As the years passed, the desire lingered just below the surface, popping up on holidays in the West Highlands or occasional camping weekends. Then in 2010, ironically thanks to the economic recession, came the opportunity to fulfil the dream. I had been running a family owned retail business operating in Falkirk. But from 2007 trading became increasingly difficult. The credit crunch saw people spending less on big household items such as carpets and furniture, the very goods on which the family business had been founded. Three years later I made the difficult decision to stop trading. Keeping this a secret while I took time to make doubly sure it was the right decision was terrible and the pressure weighed heavily on me. A summer holiday in Dumfries nearly ended in divorce. However once I had told my family, staff, customers and suppliers a great weight was lifted from my shoulders and following a final sale the business stopped trading.

Whilst searching for a new career, I realised I had an opportunity to make my escape. At the same time my kids were all now at school and that little less dependent on my wife, Nicola and I. True, I seemed to spend an increasing amount of time as a taxi driver but we had now shifted to the stage where my daughters wanted pals not parents. The guilt at the thought of leaving them all for a few weeks began to dissipate and with the big 40 just around the corner and the realisation that I wasn't getting any younger, the thirst for the big adventure loomed larger than ever.

I needed a plan. Disappearing into Glen Affric for a few weeks didn't appeal for an extended journey. Despite the beauty of the surroundings, how would I fill my time once I was there? I could climb all the hills in the locale, swim in the loch and hang out at my campsite but this lacked purpose. I wanted to undertake some form of meaningful journey in the hills. Being keen on history, I have always been fascinated with the old tracks, pathways and coffin or drove roads that criss-cross the landscape. The lesser known the path, the better as the feeling of discovery always added to the fun. To walk on an ancient pathway thinking of ancestors who traipsed the same roads for a particular purpose added another dimension to any journey. I decided then that I wanted my escape to combine history and remote terrain. I needed a substantial journey with some form of historical significance. That is where I turned to the story of Bonnie Prince Charlie and his wanderings.

Having spent a good deal of time in the north-west of Scotland, the Jacobite Rising of 1745–46 fascinated me greatly. In this area, the Prince landed and raised the Highland Clans before marching south at their head. From here, he left in 1746 having survived for five months as a fugitive after his army was defeated at the battle of Culloden. The associated monuments, cairns and caves dotted all over the Highlands made me realise the importance of the Prince to the history of the area, and it was his escape in the Highlands and Islands after the Rising failed that interested me most. Charles fought a physical and mental battle to outwit the forces seeking to apprehend him. This journey is recorded as his finest hour and consisted of exactly the type of terrain that I wanted to escape to.

With the Jacobite army soundly defeated at the Battle of Culloden, the young Prince had to move swiftly to avoid capture by the victorious troops. Riding away from the battlefield after a failed attempt to rally the troops, he headed for the west coast to try to find a ship from which to return to France. Within a couple of days of his defeat, Charles was on foot, deep in the highlands, moving from glen to glen, travelling light and living rough with just a few followers. For the next five months he remained a hunted fugitive with a £30,000 (a six figure sum in today's money) price tag on his head. Pursued by the Duke of Cumberland, the British Army and Highland Militia as well as by ships from the British Navy, Charles undertook an arduous flight across land and sea. An incredible journey stretching across the Highlands and Islands and back again as he sought to avoid capture and escape to France. Finally, after one of the most gruelling experiences anyone, never mind a royal prince, has ever had to endure, he escaped Scotland aboard a French ship from Loch nan Uamh in September 1746, intent on coming back to relieve the Highlanders of the plight in which he had left them.

This journey seemed to me to have everything I was looking for. A well-documented historical trail to follow through often remote and mountainous terrain. Lots of opportunity for wild camping in beautiful locations. A physically demanding challenge, requiring a high degree of self-sufficiency. Following in the footsteps of one of Scotland's most renowned characters there would be an opportunity to get to know the man as well as the myth. There was plenty of reading material to be getting on with, so I did my research and made a plan. There are good books detailing the Prince's escape and some authors have travelled sections of the route. But no one had attempted to recreate the journey in a single outing. I decided to make this my goal, recreating as accurately as possible his movements during the period of flight. Travelling with me would be Meg, my five-year-old border collie. In the course of the journey I would visit all the sites that Bonnie Prince Charlie frequented, including houses, castles and caves.

I dug out 1:50,000 Ordnance Survey Landranger Maps and started plotting. Having planned many hill-walking trips, the same principles still applied, although this was many times bigger than any journey I had undertaken previously. From the descriptions I had of the Prince's escape, I started to transfer his route to the map. Sometimes the planning was easy, as a more modern path or road has simply replaced the old path that the Prince followed. In fact, some sections of General Wade's roads built after the Jacobite rising of 1715 and which Charles occasionally used remain today. On other occasions following the route accurately meant foregoing paths and looking to find a realistic way through glens and across hills.

I love maps, your index finger following a route, spotting points of interest whether it is a cave, a cairn or a section of General Wade's military road. With unbounded enthusiasm I poured over maps tracing out the Prince's route. On a few occasions how he got from one location to another is unknown, but in the main I followed W.B. Blaikie's *Itinerary of Prince Charles Edward Stuart; from his landing in Scotland, 1745 to his departure in 1746* (Scottish History Society, 1897). This was constructed from first hand journals and accounts in the *Lyon in Mourning* by Bishop Forbes, published by the Scottish History Society in 1895.

Sometimes I would have to walk the modern, traffic-bearing road rather than a nearby path because that was the route the Prince took. My decision to be accurate wasn't always going to produce the best excursion! Based on previous experience and taking my backpack into consideration, I estimated that I could travel 26km (approx. 16 miles) per day. Overall, the approximate pace would be four kilometres (2.5 miles) per hour, not including rests, and on climbing days the distance would be reduced according to the total amount of height to be gained.

One day a week I would rest my legs. This was intended to be a tough physical challenge but one I was determined to enjoy. It was not a punitive speed march. During walking days I also had to retain enough energy to make camp, record my thoughts and cook a decent meal. I had been in situations before where I had arrived back at a campsite so exhausted that I had unzipped the tent, crawled in and crashed out without food or drink. Being on my own, I couldn't afford to be blasé with my well-being or timetable.

Quite soon I had a rough plan. Travelling through the Northwest Highlands, the Outer Hebrides, Skye and Raasay, I would be walking just over 800km (500 miles). Taking in a combination of modern roads, paths and trackless mountainside wherever the Prince's party had walked. There would also be 500km (300 miles) of ferry and bus journeys. Amongst the sailings made by the Prince were journeys from Arisaig to Benbecula and Elgol to Mallaig. No modern day ferries run these exact routes so I would walk to the water's edge where the Prince embarked and then take public transport to the relevant ferry port. After the ferry crossing, I would make my way to the point where the Prince landed. Reconstructing the journey in this way, I would still be walking almost exactly where the Prince walked in 1746.

In the main, I would rough camp and sleep in my tent, trying to make sure that my campsites were located in as interesting but sheltered places as possible. I would also make use of a few bothies, the odd hotel and one hostel. There are also a number of caves associated with the Prince, ranging from a tiny one near Loch Arkaig, to a more commodious affair at Glen Moriston with its own running water. I tried to organise my days so that I would end up at a cave as often as possible. Whether I would sleep in

I DON'T CARE IF BONNIE PRINCE CHARLIE'S TRAIL *DOES* COME THROUGH OUR LIVING ROOM - YE'RE NO COMIN' IN!!

Courtesy of Jim Barker

them would depend on their (and my) condition. Not only would I follow Charlie, I also hoped I would get to understand him a little better by putting myself through a very similar set of circumstances to that which he experienced. Sure, government forces weren't chasing me, and robbing a bank without a mask just to get hunted wasn't a realistic option. However, many things would be the same including the distance travelled, the terrain, the weather, the scenery, the fatigue, the midges, and the insecurity of completing the journey. As I would be alone during the journey I would also have to deal with loneliness and be almost completely self-reliant.

The overall terrain has changed very little in the intervening 266 so my experience of the route would be very similar to that of the Prince. The main exception was the time of travel. Quite often, the Prince journeyed at night and rested during the day to avoid observation. I would stick with daytime travel. Enjoying my surroundings was essential to me. Survival instinct also kicked in. Crossing unknown and rough territory at night could too easily result in a sprained ankle. Even walking on modern roads at night could be a recipe for disaster! I hoped, by following his epic route, having already done the background reading that I could get inside his head. I wanted to explore his motivation and to see if anything about this final farewell to the Highlands affected his future thinking. The rights and wrongs of the Rising of 1745–46 still spark heated debate.

Supporters would argue that he was justifiably trying to restore his family, the Stuarts, back to their rightful position as monarchs of England, Scotland and Ireland. Initially stoked with great drive and determination, he very nearly succeeded. Arriving with only a few advisors, no weapon supplies, monies or soldiers he convinced the Highland chiefs to support him, and the Rising snowballed until within five months he was at Derby and within striking distance of London. Only the absence of promised support from France, and the failure of English Jacobites to rise to the cause prevented him from claiming the throne for his father. We will never know whether this support was necessary for success, but it was certainly necessary to convince Charles' Council of War to march on to London.

Others see the Prince as a reckless youth who was wrong to start a rising with only promises of support from France and the English

Jacobites. He also lacked due regard for the consequences for the people who supported him. When things went badly, as they ultimately did, then the Highland Clans would pay a high price for supporting him. Having spoken to a quite a few people from the Highlands during research for my trip I was surprised, perhaps naively, by the strength of feeling that the Jacobite Rising of 1745 still generates. I determined to find out during my journey how Charles was viewed amongst the descendants of those who rose for the Prince and who suffered in the aftermath of Culloden as the Government dispensed fire and sword amongst the clans.

With my trip still some way off, I started to work on my fitness regime and took up running again. Using canal towpaths, old drove roads or forest tracks, I always tried to head off-road for clear air, better scenery and so that my dogs could run freely. The next step in my plan of action was to get out on the hills again. Having notched up about 150 Munros over the years, I had lost interest in doing many more as I was spending more time in the car to reach them than I was on the hill enjoying them. However, this time round I headed for the Ochil Hills, just a short drive away, refreshing map reading skills, getting used to carrying a pack again, and reminding my legs of the joys of going uphill.

With my wife, Nicola, and three young daughters to consider, disappearing for six weeks on a self-fulfilling journey seemed slightly selfish to begin with, particularly as Nicola also worked full time. Perhaps if I explained my reasoning I could just about make it fly. So one Friday night, whilst watching TV with Nicola, I gathered enough Dutch courage to blurt out my plan as fast as I possibility could.

'I am going away for a six week walk.'

'What!'

Slower this time, 'I am going away for a six week walk.'

'When?'

'Next year.'

'Who with?'

'Meg.'

'Where?'

'The Highlands.'

'Why?'

'Because I want to do something different.'

'What?'

'Follow Bonnie Prince Charlie.'

'He's deid! What about me? What about the kids? Who'll look after Ailsa? [The other dog] Who'll take the kids to school? And my fitness classes? Who'll babysit? When exactly are you going? Who's going to help me? My mother can't do any more. What about your job? HAVE YOU THOUGHT THIS THROUGH?'

All perfectly plausible questions, I just wasn't expecting them all at once.

A few weeks later I slipped into a conversation 'I need to do a practice...'

So a few months later my eldest daughter, Sophie and I completed the 98-mile West Highland Way. We carried our own gear, well not quite true, I carried my gear and I carried her gear. She was aged only 11 after all. We took seven days to complete the journey, camping out at night. The scenery was stunning, my daughter and I got on well together, I learned a few lessons for my next adventure and we raised some money for charity.

I ended up setting a target weight for my rucksack of 20kg for the main mission. I had carried 28kg on my practice expedition and it was too much. To start with, I wouldn't be carrying my daughter's gear as I had previously. Then I changed some of my older camping gear for newer lightweight versions: sleeping bag, tent, and stove. I added some extras like an inflatable mattress and a lightweight chair frame. Not necessary for a shorter trip, but essential to have some comfort for this length of journey. My sustenance would in the main be dried food and I would carry seven days' worth at a time, re-stocking either at shops or with some carefully hidden supply bags, which I would place in remote locations before I left. There would be no Highlanders out foraging for me. Keeping spare clothes down to a minimum, I cut other items from my inventory mercilessly. Happily passing some of my equipment on for Meg to carry, I brought the rucksack weight down to just less than 20kg.

Meg, my five-year-old collie, was the unfortunate victim of my campaign to cut down my backpack weight. Six weeks before, I bought a doggy rucksack and started making her go out in public with it. Dogs that we had met countless times on previous walks now started coming up to her and barking their heads off as if to say 'What the hell are you wearing that for? If Bob and Betty see you with that, they'll be buying one for me next week and then my street cred will be zip, just like yours!'

With my route planned out, feeling fit, rucksack packed and family appeased, I was ready to go.

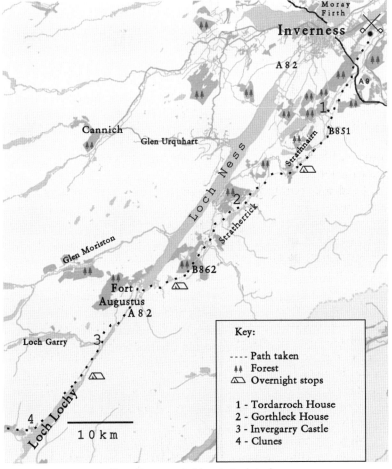

From Drummossie Moor to Loch Lochy

CHAPTER 2

From Culloden to Arisaig

THIRTY MINUTES AND it was all over. Bonnie Prince Charlie was led from Culloden field in tears, his previously unbeaten army routed. Unable to accept responsibility for defeat, he claimed he had been betrayed. In truth however, he had been determined to make a stand on this hugely unsuitable battlefield despite the pleadings of his senior military advisers. Insurmountable odds were stacked against the Jacobites and the Duke of Cumberland's government army exerted a killing blow on the rising.

The Highlanders who lined up on Drummossie Moor on 16 April 1746 were tired and hungry after an abortive attempt at ambushing Cumberland's forces the previous night. Five thousand weary men lined up on a battlefield poorly suited to them, facing 9,000 well-drilled government troops. Virtually without reply the government artillery decimated the Jacobite ranks as the men awaited the order to attack. When they eventually did charge, their lack of numbers and the poor ground prevented them from breaking the enemy's line. The Jacobites were soon swept aside by an army that outgunned them in all departments: number of troops, morale, discipline, weapons, artillery and leadership.

Now began the final act of the Jacobite Rising of 1745–46. Redcoats and Highlanders loyal to the government pursued Charles through the heather, across the hills and over the seas, determined to destroy the man who had come close to unseating the Hanoverian monarchy. Those that had supported Charles would pay a high price over the coming hours, days, weeks and months.

Today the National Trust for Scotland cares for Culloden Battlefield. It features a dominating memorial to the clans and a state of the art visitor centre; the battlefield has been restored to resemble its appearance in 1746. As I arrived, 266 years later, on a dark April morning, with a blanket of snow on the ground and an icy wind blowing across the exposed moor; it was an eerie and intimidating

A Highland Charge
Courtesy of National Trust for Scotland

place to be. I marched onto the field of battle, in the company of a small group of volunteers from the Culloden Battlefield Experience, whose attire added colour to the bleak landscape and whose cold steel helped set the scene. After just a few moments visualising the death and destruction that had stained this ground, I was ready to take my leave.

Charles' flight from the carnage took him to the houses of various allies and friends as he crossed the country, initially on horseback, seeking escape from the chasing government forces. Ending up at Arisaig on the rugged west coast he sailed for the Western Isles, hoping to charter a ship for France.

Following the Prince to the coast, I would cover a distance of 140 kilometres. Taking five days in total, the first three would be on roads and good paths giving me a chance to acclimatise to the rigours of the walk. The next two days would be through rougher territory. As O'Sullivan, one of the Prince's companions, put it, 'the cruellest road.'

With people milling around, my departure from my wife and children was a little restrained. With freezing temperatures it was also quite hasty. I exited the battlefield with a tear in my eye, a trusty

Richard Cadey from Radio Scotland as my *aide-de-campe* and Meg as my Sergeant at Arms. In line with the requests of the radio show, Richard was to carry my rucksack for the first mile of the trek. As he hoisted it on, I was delighted to hear him say that he thought the pack was heavy; and how on earth would I manage to carry it day after day? Going out jogging with a weighted rucksack had been part of my routine for the last eight weeks, in the hope that walking with it thereafter would seem like a breeze. One rainy day I had even ventured onto my running machine carrying a 20kg pack, but once the speed built up, the combined weight caused the track to come off the rollers and I slammed full throttle into the garage wall. I don't know who got the bigger surprise, the wall or me!

Richard and I walked off Drummossie Moor in a south-westerly direction, talking about the battle and its bloody aftermath. Reaching the perimeter we continued in the same direction crossing open fields, aiming for the road near which Richard's car was parked, loaded with satellite equipment to be set up for the interview. I was so nervous that I must have checked the map about 20 times. I kept imagining getting lost in the snowy fields and being late for a live interview on national radio. I could see Fred MacAulay sitting at his desk, 'Well, listeners we were due to interview Gregor Ewing today at the start of his 800km, six week walk, but he has got lost after half an hour.'

My fears were unfounded, I just needed to walk in a straight line and stay calm. We hopped over some barbed wire fence at the edge of the field, and onto the road, then headed west for just a short distance. I helped Richard get the pack off and waited nervously as he set up the communications. Putting on headphones I listened to the show before going live. Richard explained my trek to Fred and the listeners and I then answered questions about my journey. Fred was particularly taken with the fact that I had buried my food supplies for collecting en route, commenting on the fact that now I had announced it on national radio, they might not be there any longer. With the interview over I said cheerio to Richard and trotted off; looking back he was already busy dismantling the equipment.

Suddenly I was on my own and the shock hit me hard. Here I was on the start of something that I had thought about every day for over a year – an enterprise far bigger than anything I had ever attempted before. With all the publicity I had received there was no turning back. But what was I thinking about, six weeks of solo walking, and living out of a backpack and a tiny tent? I was totally inexperienced for this sort of thing. This trek was five times further than I ever been before on a single trip and that was on a way-marked path. Much of this trip was through wild terrain where almost anything could go wrong. How would I cope if it rained continuously for days on end? A minor injury in a remote place could put me in serious danger. I was used to a busy home and a busy workplace, I even liked crowded pubs. The quiet might drive me crazy. I started to panic. A wet feeling on my leg broke the spell of doom that I was casting over myself. Not an accident with my bladder surely? Oh no! My kilt was really wet too. Taking off my rucksack to allow further investigations, I discovered my drinking pouch was burst at the seams and totally useless. I turned on my phone, which was for emergency use only.

'Nicola, I need help.'

'Whaaat? You've only been away an hour!'

I could tell from the tone of her voice she was expecting something dreadful. Knowing my general clumsiness I don't think a broken leg would have surprised her. However she agreed to get me a new pouch and meet me later. She didn't sound too chuffed at my mishap, and was probably thinking 'How on earth is he going to cope for six weeks when he's calling me after an hour.'

I continued on towards Balvraid Farm, three kilometres west of the battlefield. In this vicinity the Prince was dissuaded from attempting to rally the clans and charge back onto the battlefield. This would undoubtedly have led to certain death.

Here it was that Gillies MacBean, a relative giant in those times at 6'4", unable to keep up with his fleeing clan, rested his injured body against a farm building and awaited his fate, determined not to sacrifice his life without a fight. They say that he killed 13 Hanoverian soldiers before he was overcome; some bright spark eventually clambered onto the roof of the building to successfully attack him. Even then he was found alive afterwards and hidden with straw, but died before any further assistance reached him.

Once dissuaded, the Prince made his way to the Fords of Faillie where he crossed the river Nairn. The area is known as Scatraig or the scattering because here after the battle many of the highland clans broke up and dispersed. Here Charles also dismissed the cavalry that had escorted him thus far and with only a few companions his flight truly began. Meanwhile those that were not so fortunate to make it this far were treated in a barbaric fashion. The wounded highlanders were left initially on Culloden Moor while the government troops, having secured the battlefield, made for Inverness. Many Jacobites or suspected sympathisers were caught and killed on the way. Over the next two days squads of soldiers were sent out to kill any injured rebels either at Culloden or in the surrounding area. They splashed each other with the blood of the slain earning the Duke of Cumberland the sobriquet of 'Butcher'. Houses containing wounded soldiers were burned down, the occupants prevented from escaping as soldiers barred the doors.

Leaving the farm at Balvraid, I too headed for the Fords of Faillie following the B851. Snow covered fields surrounded me, the silence was broken only by the occasional car passing. Meg walked contentedly on the lead. This was to be a big test of our relationship and Nicola had warned me not to bother coming back if anything happened to the dog! During the trip I wanted to get on better terms with Meg. I had never really accepted her properly, having bowed to my families' demands for another Collie. Having a dog already, someone had said to me 'You have bought a pet for your pet, you must be mad.' This stuck and although obedient, Meg's training wasn't as good as I would have liked it to be. I realised I had probably been a little hard on her and not given her the proper attention. Here was my chance to bond with her.

Crossing the busy A9 dual carriageway at Daviot was my biggest challenge so far. There were no cars going anywhere near the speed limit, they were all going about 50km per hour over it. I sat down and took my first rest by a church although I had no need for divine intervention at this early stage. The minister walked past with his terrier, who came over for a sniff of Meg. 'That's a nice collie, not like that one down the road,' he said to his pet. I never thought any more of the remark; I was making sure I wasn't being immodest with my kilt. Flashing at a minister could turn my journey into a manhunt after all.

A few minutes later I was walking down the only street in the village when a collie type dog in one of the gardens started going mental and barking menacingly. As I passed the open gate, the dog came flying out of the garden snapping at Meg. I pulled on the lead to get her away but the dog was nipping at her rear and rucksack, barking furiously. I tried to kick the dog as we backed off but it was too fast for me. The woman of the house was by now rattling on a window, whether at the dog or me I wasn't sure, but I felt like rattling her. Once we got far enough away from the garden the dog backed off, having defended its territory. I was furious with her letting her dog behave that way. Next time though, I would listen when someone provided me with a piece of local knowledge.

The footpath marked on my map taking me from the minor road to the bridge over the River Nairn was overgrown and obviously rarely used, a barely-surviving section of General Wade's road. I crossed the old bridge just upstream of where the Prince crossed, at the Ford of Faillie and sauntered along the B851 continuing my travels through Strathnairn wondering when my replacement pouch would turn up. When my car came flying round a corner towards me and screeched to a halt, Nicola was stressed out to the maximum, having got lost on the back roads on the south side of Loch Ness. Saying cheerio to my wife and kids once more, this time it was Nicola who rushed off as she tried to find her way back to Inverness.

I headed for Tordarroch, the very same house that the Prince approached seeking shelter, although it seemed far too close to the battlefield for my liking. Perched on an embankment overlooking the river, it was a beautifully restored three-storey tower house. Just as in 1746, the owner of Tordarroch house was not in. Charles finding the home of Angus Shaw unoccupied pressed on, making his first stop at Gorthleck House further along the road.

In the late afternoon, the sun came out and provided some brightness and warmth to lift my now flagging spirits. Low in the sky and shining though the pine trees, it reflected off the snowy fields giving an alpine look and feel to the valley.

On hearing wolf like howls coming from some large pens nearby, I thought I was in the Twilight Zone.

The owner came to see who was causing the commotion and when he saw I was a hiker he recommended a B&B along the road, but I

Tordarroch House

explained that after lugging the tent around all day I was going to use it. He warned me where not to camp in the vicinity, explaining that some of the local landowners were a bit fierce with people wild camping. Moving swiftly on, I asked him about his large dogs pacing up and down within. He explained that they were Mamuts, a hybrid breed of wolf and dog.

As I passed Loch Ruthven Nature reserve I was able to identify a couple of black-throated divers. My brief ornithology lesson from a friend that I thought had gone in one ear and out the other had paid dividends. I had intended carrying a bird watchers book to make up for my ignorance but the book was discarded at one of the numerous rucksack weigh-ins.

Getting back to wolves, the last one in this area was killed in 1700 by a lady on the slopes above Loch Ruthven. She had gone to borrow a girdle for baking from a neighbour, when she came upon a hungry wolf. She lamped the poor beast with the pan and delivered a killing blow. Can you imagine what a 21st century person would do in that position? Laugh, cry, wibble or most likely hit themselves with the pan to escape from their misery!

By 7.30pm I was shattered. My body said 'stop,' my stomach said 'feed me now,' and my shoulders said 'we give in, whatever we have done wrong we are sorry and we won't ever do it again. Just please remove these straps.' Since 11am I had covered nearly 24km, which was a credible distance for my first day. I decided to camp just off the road behind a ruined cottage, wary of any fierce landowners. Clearing the area of a thin layer of snow I hurriedly tried to set up the tent and ended up bursting a hole in the flysheet with one of the poles. Great start, ripping the tent on the first night. Sitting outside, I was halfway through heating my evening meal when it started to rain. Could things get any worse? Crabbit now and tiring fast, I finished cooking and crawled into my tent where there was just enough room for Meg, the rucksack and me. I took a few notes and fell fast asleep, pen in hand, whilst the rain pee'd through the hole.

I awoke with another damp patch on my body. I was losing confidence in my bodily functions. I knew what the next stage of this downward spiral was likely to be and I didn't like the thought of it one little bit. I was wearing a kilt and there was no protection for those below. Another worry was that my fancy-ass, super-light, ultra warm but don't-let it-get-wet sleeping bag was now soaked through.

Thus, I was up early. There was no rain so I dismantled the tent by which time the rain had started again. Foregoing breakfast until it eased off I continued on the road, the Great Glen and Loch Ness were just a stone's throw away to the north but were not in sight. At 8am I was peering over some trees toppled by recent storms into the grounds of Aberarder house. The house itself looked old but I didn't go in and ask if it was contemporary with Bonnie Prince Charlie as knocking on someone's door so early would warrant a reply entirely unconnected with the age of the house. Charles hadn't stopped here so I didn't delay and carried on, although I found out later that the original house does remain. The ground changed to heather clad moorland as I rounded a small hill taking me out of Strathnairn and into Stratherrick, a wide, shallow valley running in a south-easterly direction below the Great Glen.

As it was still raining heavily I took shelter in some woods by Loch Mhor to have a hot breakfast. Overlooking the loch is Gorthleck Mains, a two storey whitewashed house where Bonnie Prince Charlie met Lord Lovat, the 79-year-old Chief of Clan Fraser who was staying with his kinsman. Both wily and clever, Lord Lovat was a ruthless individual without principle when it came to achieving his own interests. He had spent a lifetime building up his estates and power. Throughout his life he had shifted allegiances in order to end up on the winning side. Doubtless he would have been appalled that a defeated Charles was at his door.

Charles had sought Lovat's support earlier in the campaign, but as usual Lovat played both sides, sending his son with a strong force of clansmen to support Charles, whilst proclaiming his favour for the status quo to the authorities. Now he offered Charles hospitality and duplicitous advice. Fight on, he advised, after all Robert the Bruce had lost 11 battles before his fortunes turned for the better. However the only realistic fighting option open to Charles was to wage a guerrilla war from a secure mountain base. But the wily Lord cautioned that a mountain campaign could not be sustained without money or food, of which Charles had neither.

From Gorthleck, Charles' *aide-de-campe* wrote a letter to Cluny MacPherson, the leader of Clan Chattan and Charles' friend. He stated that the army was to re-group at Fort Augustus and that the Prince had plans to avenge Culloden. Then around midnight (still the same day as the abortive night march to Nairn prior to the battle) Charles set off again, making for Fort Augustus. Possibly Cumberland's Dragoons were close on his tail. Legend has it that he jumped from an upper window at the rear of the house to escape. No one was in at the house when I called, so I was unable to find out if the current occupier would let me replicate this dramatic exit.

The majority of the defeated Jacobites had made for Ruthven in Badenoch thinking that was the rallying place. So did Lord George Murray, the Prince's general for almost the entire campaign. Lord George had been in command at the Jacobite victories at Prestonpans and Falkirk. He was responsible for the strategy that took the Jacobite army to Derby, within striking distance of London. He had also organised the retreat from Derby and the small victories that had taken place afterwards, including the skirmish at Clifton. The Princes had a fractious relationship with the overbearing Lord George, which had eventually collapsed prior to the defeat at Culloden. The Prince then took personal command of the army with advice from his Irish Adjutant-General, O'Sullivan.

Gorthleck House

Lord George and his force had retired in good order from the battle. Meeting Cluny McPherson and 500 of his clansmen on the way, Lord Murray had asked him to provide rear guard cover for the shattered army. Cluny in turn gave the Prince's letter to Lord George who was stupefied that Charles had made for Lochaber while the army made for Badenoch. On the day after the battle Lord George penned a letter resigning his commission and blaming the Prince for all the ills that had befallen the rising and the army.

By 20 April, the army had dispersed at Ruthven. This was for one of two reasons, either because the Prince had ordered every man for himself as some accounts say, or because no word was received from the Prince. The Highlands were now completely unprotected, giving the Duke of Cumberland's forces free rein to visit their depredations on any area suspected of supporting or collaborating with the Prince. In the months following the battle, rape, murder and pillage were inflicted upon the Highlanders on a scale that no Jacobites had foreseen. Cumberland aimed to destroy the ability of the Highland Chiefs to wage war.

Leaving Gorthleck House, I followed the minor road, the B862 and reached the old bridge at Dalcrag, over the Allt an Loin (Burn of the marsh). The rain had ceased and using the bridge as shelter from the wind I stopped for lunch in a field overlooking the river. Whilst trying to light my stove I managed somehow to set it on fire. Flames were pouring forth and spouting upwards. I knocked the stove over but this set the grass on fire. I reached over to turn off the gas but the flames kept spouting out. The next stage was to launch the stove into the river but thankfully the flames at last disappeared. I stomped on the burning grass. If the ground hadn't been so wet I could have been dealing with a blazing inferno. Apart from the fright, and the whiff of burnt hair from my mutilated brows, I was fine. I reached for some dried fruit for lunch. Just as I was recovering my poise, Meg came wandering over minus her rucksack. I now ran up and down the riverside like a headless chicken searching frantically, shouting for it to return, as if I expected an answer, 'Cooee I'm over here.' Eventually I found it, precariously perched on the bank, just a few centimetres from disappearing forever into the fast flowing water. Meg must have been leaning forward to drink when it slipped forward over her head. Giving herself a good shake she had rid herself of it completely. I looked to St Johns Cemetery over the bridge and wondered if the spirits were playing games with me.

Including the burst water pouch and the torn tent that was four mishaps, or near mishaps in just over 24 hours. I couldn't go on at that rate. In a few days I would be heading into remote territory where there was no one to hear you scream.

Still muttering, 'Sheer bloody carelessness' a somewhat familiar phrase from childhood, I continued along the modern road, which had been built on top of General Wade's road. I arrived at the village of Whitebridge where the original humpback bridge built in 1732 still remains. No doubt Charles used this bridge as he headed for Fort Augustus. The bridge is in a dangerous condition and no longer in use. It had done its job and didn't owe anybody anything having been the main crossing for 200 years. It was fenced off to prevent use, although I could slip round the fence if required. Whilst I weighed up the pros and cons, a teenage girl came out of a nearby house, brushed past me and walked right over it. Feeling like an idiot for hesitating I followed her over.

It was now a long straight walk in heavy rain along Stratherrick, where the road eventually climbed up to a height of 400m on the

Whitebridge

slopes of Suidehe Chumain. In English this translates as Cumein's Seat, named for a 7th century Abbot of Iona who founded nearby Fort Augustus. This was my first climb, a long one and a bit of a slog with the rucksack weighing heavy at the end of a long day. Reaching the top I was greeted with fine views over towards the Great Glen as well as back along the territory I had just traversed. The rain had washed away the snow and now that it had stopped, the weather brightened and a few rays of sunshine were peeping through. Descending towards Loch Tarff, Meg was beginning to struggle, unable to keep up with my pace. Not knowing what else to look for, I checked her paws. They seemed fine and she wasn't limping. It was maybe just tiredness, as she had walked 28km today with five kilograms on her back. I removed her rucksack, annoyed that I would have to carry her pack as well as my own. The dog was supposed to lighten my load, not the other way around. Here I was buckling at the knees while she now trotted along quite the thing.

Before long the land opened out before me and below was a small loch with tiny, tree-filled islands, surrounded by low hills. The distant

Looking back over Stratherrick

hills of Glendoe Forest made a lovely backdrop. Camping on the north bank, I managed to use the stove successfully and satisfy my hunger. For the first time in a good few days I was able to relax. The frenzied final preparations and the last minute worries were behind me. I had made a confident start to the walk and was bang on schedule. My wet tent, sleeping bag and waterproofs were drying nicely in the evening sun. Meg and I were both shattered but lying outside just looking at the scenery was bliss. The adventure had truly begun,

Turning on my mobile phone to report home, I received some well-wishing texts. One from my friend Gary offered the following advice first advocated by William Shakespeare, 'Our doubts are traitors, and make us lose the good we oft might win, by fearing to attempt.' He was right; plenty of people had been sceptical that I could attempt this, but even in the wee sma' hours I had remained determined.

Early next morning Loch Tarff was completely still, the surface reflecting perfectly the grey early morning light. Getting back on the road I crossed Glen Doe before descending to Fort Augustus. Arriving at this fine little village I had a lovely vantage point for looking down the dark peat stained waters of Loch Ness. At 37km long, Loch Ness fills the northern third of the Great Glen, a geological fault line dividing Scotland in two and running in a diagonal across the country from

Loch Tarff

Inverness to Fort William. Fort Augustus was originally called Cill Chuimein, cell of the Church of Cumein. Following the 1715 Jacobite Rising a fort was built, of which one of the original barracks walls can be seen behind the Lovat Arms Hotel. A new fort nearer to Loch Ness (for easier re-supplying by boat) was completed in 1742 and named after the second son of King George II, none other than William Augustus, Duke of Cumberland.

Earlier in the 1745 campaign, the Jacobites had attacked the castle and blown up the powder magazine wreaking extensive damage. It was rebuilt after the Rising, but in 1876 the disused fort was encompassed within the walls of a Benedictine Abbey. The Abbey was a fine collection of buildings built around a 30m quadrangle. In 1993 the demise of the buildings for religious and educational purposes led to the abbey being converted into a private holiday apartment complex. I went to see the remaining bastion of the newer fort, the surviving walls now being a part of the buildings that make up the holiday complex. Sneaking along a private path I soon saw what I was looking for, four metre high walls that make up the northeast corner of this spectacular group of buildings. The unadorned walls are in stark contrast when all around is decorative and elaborate.

When Prince Charles arrived here, he did not wait long to see if

Former Abbey at Fort Augustus

any remnants of his army would catch him up and so he rode on, making for Invergarry Castle. This would seem to be the most obvious evidence that his mind was made up to abandon the rising and return to France.

Following in his wake, I took the route of General Wade's road, which is now the A82 heading for Spean Bridge. To avoid the traffic my plan had been to follow the dismantled railway, which runs alongside the road. This line was dismantled after World War II but had previously connected Fort Augustus with Spean Bridge. It was marked on my map, but when I had checked with the assistant in the tourist office at Fort Augustus, she had not heard of anyone using this track for a while and thought it would be too overgrown to walk on. I thought I would try it anyway as being the lesser of two evils when compared to the road.

As I left Fort Augustus I swapped the pavement for the old railway track. It started out fine. At this point the line had been cut through higher ground and there were steep banks on either side. Apart from a few trees the route of the old track was clear, and for the first time Meg was off the lead.

However my luck didn't last, that would have been too easy. I resorted to the road to avoid what I thought was an encampment of travellers caravans at Loch Uanagan. This was the first time I had walked with Meg on such a busy road and it was a bit of a shock. Having to step off the road and onto the verge each time a car appeared in front of me soon became very annoying. In general the verge was too narrow to walk along, so I had to step back onto the tarmac until the next car came hurling towards me at 60 miles an hour plus. Before I had a head on collision with a car, I clambered over a stone dyke to try and find the route of the old railway track again. Fighting my way through gorse bushes and dense thickets of birch trees I did manage to locate it. At this point it was almost completely obscured, but I stuck with it and it gradually improved. For a stretch it cut through a conifer plantation and the route became a good forest track. The last few kilometres had really taken a lot out of me so I stopped here for porridge. Meg wolfed her breakfast down, then sat and stared intently at me as I cooked and ate mine. This normally unnerves and then starts to annoy me but I was too tired to care. She was in a worse state though and fell asleep whilst sitting up. What on earth was I putting this dog through?

Further along the track I reached some high fences that were blocking my path and going to be a real challenge to get over. On the other side cattle were feeding from a trailer filled with hay, so I gave up with the railway line; this was far too much hassle. I had ignored local knowledge again. Had I walked along by the canal as suggested then I would have had a pleasant stroll. There was still a fence, albeit a lower one, preventing me from reaching the road and here I encountered yet another hitch. Halfway over I got my kilt stuck on the barbed wire and gave the poor picnickers in their campervan a nasty shock. Cucumber sandwiches followed by a full moon from an unshaven dirty and hairy arsed desperado.

Near the tearoom at Aberchalder a group of ladies from Poland were waiting for Meg and I. They wanted to have their pictures taken with us. Will wonders never cease; we were a tourist attraction! Meg and I could now feature on the same list as Stirling Castle, Holyrood Palace and Baxter's soup factory!

By lunchtime I had covered about 13km and having reached Aberchalder, I crossed the River Oich heading for Invergarry Castle. Crossing the river there is a swing bridge to allow canal traffic to pass and an older suspension bridge, now just a tourist attraction. This 50m bridge built in 1854 is a nice photo stop but otherwise not much use as crossing it leads to a private estate where your entry is barred. Bah!

Next up was a section of forest path running down the side of Loch Oich and avoiding the busy road. Those doing The Great Glen Way, a long distance trail connecting Fort William and Inverness, may use this stretch of path. The Great Glen Way is 126km long and can be completed, on foot, horseback, bike, mobility scooter or even canoe. I followed the track through the forest, enjoying the fresh, sharp smell of the pine needles. On my map was marked a footpath coming off the main drag and leading down towards Invergarry castle, but when I arrived at the spot to join this path, there were no way-markers and the track was overgrown. I was suspicious, but there was no alternative so I pushed on downhill. Soon the path was barely visible and then all of a sudden it ended completely at a wall of gorse and rhododendron bushes. I couldn't believe this was happening; there must be some sort of law against inaccurate maps. I could feel anger building and adrenalin starting to flow.

Like a madman I fought, crawled and squeezed my way downhill until I could hear the traffic of the nearby road. Perched on top of a giant fallen tree I was trying to jump over some dense foliage to another horizontal trunk protruding from the undergrowth when I stopped for a timeout to catch my breath and take in what was happening. The adrenalin ebbed away and I realised this was getting dangerous. I retreated to find an easier escape. However as I tried to back up, the cords from my tent, which I was stupidly drying on the back of my rucksack, got tangled in the branches. I was precariously balanced and couldn't pull too hard for fear of ripping the tent. Carefully I removed my rucksack without falling from the wooden precipice and untangled the cords, swearing at myself in the most explicit way. The tent should have been put away as soon as the going got tough.

Eventually extricating myself I turned back uphill and tried another direction, and after a few false starts I eventually found a way through the thick undergrowth that still allowed me to keep my feet on the ground. Shocked and scratched, I emerged onto the road once more. I checked things over and noticed I had lost the bite valve off my bloody drinking pouch. Screw it, I would manage. I headed onto a side road crossing the River Garry where canoeists were having a fabulous time. Lucky them. The spectators on the bridge parted to let me pass, I had a thunderous look on my face and I resembled Treebeard with branches sticking out everywhere. I stormed on past the Invergarry hotel and then onto the ruins of Invergarry Castle where I threw down my rucksack.

The five-storey L-Plan castle with a six-storey tower overlooks Loch Oich from its position on top of the Rock of the Raven. The owners, the MacDonnells of Glengarry, had been staunch Jacobites throughout the risings. This family gave complete commitment to the cause. The chief had declared for Charlie and his second son Angus had fought throughout the campaign. Unfortunately Angus was killed after the battle of Falkirk in an accident with a supposedly unloaded pistol.

The Chief's oldest son Alastair was imprisoned in the tower of London for the duration of the rising where he was 'turned' by the London government and between 1750 and 1754 acted as a spy on Bonnie Prince Charlie and his court.

The Prince arrived at Invergarry Castle to find it empty of all people, furnishings and food. He stayed overnight though and a decent meal was enjoyed when his servant Ned Burke found a couple of salmon trapped in a net in the river. The following day he resumed his journey on what would be his last day on horseback for five months. The Prince's party – now consisting of just O'Sullivan, Burke, an Irish soldier called O'Neill and a priest, Alexander MacLeod – didn't stop until they reached the far end of Loch Arkaig. Shortly afterwards the Duke of Cumberland's men burned the castle and ever since it has remained a burned out shell, although the ruins have been stabilised in the last few years.

After lunch, I had calmed down and headed along Loch Oich, following the main road. This was a dangerous journey and I regretted not finding my way back on to the Great Glen Way at Invergarry village… Hemmed in by the loch and the steep hillside there was no walkway alongside the narrow road and few places to step off, when cars and large tourist filled buses zoomed by.

Near the southern end of the loch is a captivating monument which marks the location of the Well of the Seven Heads. In 1663 young MacDonnell gave a banquet to celebrate becoming chief of the clan. During an argument Alexander MacDonald and his six sons who

Invergarry Castle

desired the chieftainship killed him and his brother. Two years later with legal permission in the form of a 'letter of fire and sword,' a party of 50 men killed the seven murderers at their homes and cut off their heads for evidence of completion. The decapitated heads were washed in the well here before they were shown to the chief at Invergarry Castle. The story was confirmed in the 19th century when headless corpses were discovered in a nearby mound during the construction of the monument.

From the monument, thankfully there was a pavement along the final stretch of Loch Oich. A quiet side road alongside the Caledonian Canal took me past the three houses of the fabulously named Balmaglaster and on towards the north shores of Loch Lochy. Here in July 1544 the Battle of the Shirts took place, so called because due to the heat, the highlanders removed their plaids and fought only in their shirts. Three hundred Frasers fought a combined host of 500 MacDonalds and Camerons. Even for the times it was an extremely brutal affair and only four Frasers and eight of their opponents survived the battle.

Crossing the canal, I pitched my tent near Laggan Locks and waited in the evening sunshine for the arrival of my family, my mouth watering at the thought of a fish supper. The day had been a bit of an emotional roller coaster and I knew that seeing my family would help. I am not normally emotional but everything was getting bottled up and even on this relatively well-populated part of my journey I wasn't really bumping into anyone that I could talk to. A long solo walk was a new experience for me so there were bound to be problems.

Well of Seven Heads

Nicola, the kids, my in-laws Bobby and Janet, and Ailsa my other collie arrived with the longed-for fish supper, a food parcel and spare socks. After scoffing down the food I managed to hold myself together as I talked, and I felt a lot better. The tears welling up behind my eyes went back down below. The kids were in high spirits and running riot round about me, Bobby and Janet relaxed in the evening sun and Nicola examined Meg for ticks.

I had brought Meg back from the West Highland way with a dozen or more sheep/deer ticks, so this time I had been well warned to check for them. Of course I hadn't got round to it. When Nicola started shouting I guessed she had found a few. When she kept shouting I went over to take a look. Meg had large welts on her undercarriage, behind her front legs. They had been weeping and looked a mess. With the rucksack straps rubbing against them, she must have been in agony. And there was me pulling on her lead last night trying to make her keep up. Call myself a dog lover?

I got the fright of my life seeing her condition and I was warned to keep a better eye on her or she was getting pulled from the expedition. I promised to do better and obviously at the very least I would carry her stuff for a while. Already I knew Meg was essential company for me, and the dog's name was in the title of my book. 'Charlie and Me' sounded more like a drugs trip. To make space in my rucksack for

Meg's gear, I gave Nicola some non-essential stuff including my fishing gear and a lightweight camping chair that had cost me £30. Thirty quid for two bits of aluminium that you somehow wrapped your sleeping mat in to make a chair. They certainly saw me coming that day. The fishing gear didn't weigh much but I got rid of it because of guilt. I felt guilty as hell the way I had treated Meg and I had to have some form of penance. When Nicola and the kids left, I vented my upset feelings by doing a moon worshippers dance around the picnic table.

A text from Gary, 'they fail, and they alone, who have not striven.' (Thomas Bailey Aldrich 1836–1907)

'I'm failing Gary, I'm failing, help, help, help.'

The following morning I kept my worries about Meg under control as I rose early and was back on the trail for 7.30am. I had intended to walk about 30km although this seemed ambitious given the conditions, a depressing triumvirate of rain, wind and mist. The plan was to walk in a south-westerly direction following Loch Lochy and then leaving the Great Glen I would head west along the shore of Loch Arkaig, getting as close as my legs would take me to Strathan at the head of the Loch. I crossed the Kilfinnan burn, past the ancient graveyard of the MacDonnell's of Glengarry and followed Loch Lochy on a good track. Soon there were conifer plantations on either side, and high above the big and bulky Munros of Sron a Choire Ghairbh (Nose of the rough corrie) and Meall na Teanga (Hill of the tongue) dominated the locale.

Without the rucksack and free of the lead, Meg seemed quite happy as she ran back and forth and exploring the territory as we went along. Phew! The rain got heavier and the mist lower as I trundled along and I was feeling the extra weight of my pack with more food and Meg's rucksack inside. At least the forest gave me a bit of shelter but the path became a bit monotonous and recognising a tree pipit and a pine marten scat were the highlights of this section. Imagine a jobby being the highlight of your walk; come on!

On the far side of the loch was the Letterfinlay Lodge Hotel. Donald MacCulloch in *Romantic Lochaber, Arisaig and Morar* (originally printed in 1931 but a must for the general history of the area) tells the story of the original Inn, now a private home on the main road between Fort William and Spean Bridge. In 1746 40 wounded

Highlanders rested there after Culloden. Their wounds got the better of them and they travelled no further. The innkeeper, fearful of government reprisals for sheltering Jacobites, threw the bodies into Loch Lochy, where some of the corpses were later washed ashore at Clunes Bay. I have to wonder how 40 wounded men got this far and then were unable to continue. I reached the township of Clunes just north of the bay, comprising of a small cluster of log cabins and forestry commission houses.

In 1745, Cameron of Clunes was too old to join in the rising, but his four sons turned out for the Prince. Three survived whilst one was killed at the battle of Prestonpans. The father's house was burned, his animals slaughtered and his crops destroyed by Cumberland's troops during the pacification after Culloden. Leaving the Great Glen, I headed west along the Dark Mile, so called because of the dense trees that used to overhang the road, blocking out the light. Nowadays they are a little further back from the road. Three kilometres later I reached the spectacular Chi-aig waterfalls, and during a brief dry spell, I had lunch at a picnic bench with the roaring thunder of the water as a backdrop. The story goes that a local witch accused of a crime that she probably didn't commit, was chased over the falls and drowned in a large black pool, forever after known as the Witches Cauldron.

Back on my journey I continued on to remote Loch Arkaig. There are only a handful of farms along its 19km length, which are served by the minor road running along the north shore. This replaced the old track that the Prince would have followed. With dark skies above the loch looked sullen, brooding and expectant. Watching little dinghies with fishermen and fly rods, I walked passed a rocky outcrop called Rubha Cheanna Mhuir (Point of the Head of the Loch), and one and a half kilometres later I was on a section of the road historically known as the Straight Mile. The gently sloping hillside above is known as Culcairn's Brae after the following incident.

In the aftermath of the rising, a party of soldiers heading west along the loch came upon a young Highlander, Alexander Cameron, who was carrying a gun. The officer, a Captain Grant, approached on his white horse to find out why this had not been surrendered to the authorities. The Highlander said that he was on his way to hand in the

The Dark Mile ahead

gun. This excuse was not accepted and the Captain ordered him to be tied to a tree and shot.

The young man's father swore vengeance, and when he heard that the soldiers were returning, waited on the hillside above the spot where his son was killed. As the platoon passed along the Straight Mile he shot dead the officer riding a white horse.

Unfortunately, he shot the wrong officer. Two parties of soldiers had met near the head of the loch and the officers for some reason had swapped horses. The man shot was Captain George Munro of Culcairn, notorious for burning Cameron of Lochiel's house at nearby Achnacarry. This was the second significant Munro to be killed by a Cameron during the rising. Colonel Robert Munro, chief of the clan, had been killed by the Camerons at the Battle of Falkirk in January 1746. The Munros had sworn vengeance on the Camerons afterwards.

By the time I was halfway along the loch, the weather had deteriorated further. The gusting wind was creating waves on the loch and horizontal rain was driving into my face. It was Easter Sunday, I could have been eating chocolate, or rolling eggs with the kids, but I had no time for regrets, my concentration was focused on getting out of the rain. I aimed for some forestry just a few kilometres from the end of the loch. Here I could set up my tent in relative shelter. I spent ages trying to pick a site for the tent and when I did select a spot the space between the trees was too small and I was fiddling with the tent for what seemed like an age. I switched on my phone and received another inspiring text, 'I was never afraid of failure, for I would sooner fail than not be among the best.' (John Keats 1795–1821)

My tent pitch turned out to be disastrous. I couldn't stretch or turn during the night without touching its drooping wet sides. Because of the slope, I kept sliding off my sleeping mat, finding myself either against the tent sides once more or against the damp, smelly dog. To complete my misery the trees above creaked relentlessly in the wind and I lay waiting to be crushed.

The weather was bright and dry in the morning, and I looked forward to leaving the road and heading into the hills, at last. My mood was upbeat considering the poor sleep I had. Meg seemed fine as well, her welts plastered with antiseptic cream. Two kilometres from the end of the loch I came to Murlaggan, a holiday cottage. At a hut here on 8 May 1746, an attempt at raising a new body of men was agreed upon by a number of Jacobite Chiefs. The objective

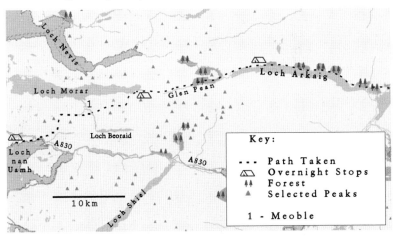

Towards Arisaig

primarily was to protect themselves and their lands from the worst of the government's retribution. There was money now to pay for armed bodies of men because the highlanders had a large quantity of gold at their disposal. On 30 April, two weeks after Culloden, two French ships, the *Mars* and the *Bellona* had landed 35,000 Louis d'or gold coins to help finance the Rising, not realising that Charles had already been defeated.

As I continued along the road the view towards the end of Loch Arkaig was beautiful. Further on a layer of mist remained in remote Glen Pean, which was towered over by steep sided, snow-capped mountains. Nearby, water was rushing off the slopes after last night's downpour.

Reaching Strathan, I was at the end of the loch and the end of the road. In this vicinity Bonnie Prince Charlie stayed overnight with Donald Cameron. The house remained until 1897 until it was destroyed by fire along with the bed in which the Prince slept. The following afternoon, Charles set off on foot with his few companions along Glen Pean, heading for the coast where he hoped to find a ship to take him to France.

Now I was more or less travelling on equal terms with the prince, I could sympathise more with the rigours of the journey. Let the wildness begin.

I entered Glen Pean on a track through a forest plantation, hemmed in by tightly bunched conifer trees, a narrow corridor of light above. After an hour I left the forest behind as the path descended down to the river and continued along the floor of the glen. With Glen Pean bothy just ahead, I was flirting with the path trying to keep my feet dry and ended up straying too far from it, stepping into a bog, instantly sinking right up to my waist. Meg had sailed straight over what looked like a grassy area and hurrying on to try to escape the oncoming rain, I hadn't given the ground due consideration. I couldn't believe the speed with which it happened. Acutely aware of the weight of my pack I turned around, sinking further as I did so, and grabbed some vegetation. I heaved my upper body bit by bit onto firm ground, adrenalin reserves kicked into action once more. Once I reached tipping point I kicked my legs like a landed fish flips its tail and I was

Inside Glen Pean Bothy

quickly out of the mire. Only then did visions of sinking without trace below the surface flood my mind.

Soaking wet below, shocked from my immersion and with the heavens opening, I shambled forward to the little stone cottage. The door opened to a large room with a concrete floor. Dripping wet I staggered in and the cold hit me like a bolt from the blue. Without further ado I stripped off my wet boots and clothes. The bothy had two large rooms with steep wooden steps leading to a large sleeping area in the roof space. The room I sat in was about five metres by four metres with a large fireplace and a stack of wood. It was furnished with a few chairs, a table, an old bus seat and a rather ominous looking metal bunk bed. Thankful for the refuge, I stripped off to dry out. I didn't have time to make a fire but after a hot lunch, a hot coffee and a change of clothes, I was ready to continue.

Of the afternoon I expected nothing too demanding, as it was only eight kilometres to another shelter, Oban bothy, where I could get a proper fire going and dry out all my gear. How wrong I was!

The sun came out, and all was well with the world once more, as I started my afternoon's walk. I followed a footpath along the narrow valley with steep sided mountains on either side. The unmistakable pointy tip of the Corbett, An Stac was visible through the gap at the end of the glen, whilst underfoot the recent deluge had caused the river to flood the entire valley floor.

I arrived at Lochan Leum an t-Sagairt (Little Loch of the Priests Jump), which filled the valley floor and on either side of it the hillsides were incredibly steep. A lovely sight, but completely blocking my progress westwards. Without swimming or climbing hundreds of feet up either of the steep sides it looked impassable. I tried the north side first, but the water was too deep to wade along the edge and when I climbed up onto the hillside it soon became a cliff side and perilous. I turned back to try the south shore, and here Meg was my saviour, finding a path not too far above the loch. It was however, extremely narrow, slippery and steep and I was finding keeping my balance difficult with the heavy pack, the sheer drops into the water making me

Lochan Leum an t-Sagairt

54

sweat profusely. While Meg kept going I knew the path continued and my confidence began to rise. Then she stopped and turned to look back at me. 'What can I do, you've got four legs and an empty rucksack,' I shouted, panicking a little. I caught up with her to find that the path zigzagged back on itself, which she hadn't noticed. When I continued she brushed past me to take the lead again.

Looking back at my journal I had noted that I didn't want it to get any scarier than that. To be honest I was out of practice with challenging hill walking especially with a heavy pack. My recent practice days in the Ochil Hills and elsewhere had probably been a little bit tame, but I had got through it and I was boosted by the small achievement. Surefootedness with my pack, and a head for heights would surely follow, as I got further into the walk. I really appreciated Meg's help on this occasion; she had shown her worth. Now it was my turn to be more understanding and appreciate how steadfast and loyal she was.

Travelling along the riverbed again, I lost all discipline in trying to keep my feet dry. The river curved this way and that along the valley floor, and I had to cross it a few times, wading up to my knees in a blasé fashion. The only consideration given was trying to find a section that Meg too would be able to cross at. Ahead, a herd of red deer were watching me, a waterfall was coming down one of the rocky hillsides, and I caught occasional glimpses of the snow-covered peaks high above. Despite the wet feet, it was a great place to be. The glen continued to funnel towards its head. I reached a large cluster of giant boulders strewn across a narrow pass that blocked my progress. This landscape was truly astounding, unchanged and unspoiled over thousands of years. If a pterodactyl had flown over my head I wouldn't have batted an eyelid.

I climbed over some of these boulders and squeezed between others. On occasion the going was too difficult for Meg and I had to lift her between rocks. Facing me next was tiny Lochan Dubh, again with what looked like unclimbable walls on either side.

Without due regard for the map hanging round my neck, I carried on thoughtlessly. I walked along the water's edge, first hopping between rocks then ploughing through the water. I remembered that a previous Prince Charles enthusiast Steve Lord had come this way and walked along the side of this little lochan. The walls got steeper though and

Boulder fall in Glen Pean

the water deeper so I was soon wading along with the water up to the tops of my thighs, shouting on the dog, trying desperately to keep my electronic gear dry. Meg wasn't as stupid as me and when I found a place to get out of the water for a breather, I turned and called to her repeatedly but there was no sign of her. Then I heard tumbling rocks and panicked. Dropping the pack I waded all the way back through the water to the beginning of the loch, shouting Meg's name but not seeing her. This time I took a higher path and to my utter relief I found her perched on a rock high above the lochan. She had probably been there all the time, watching me plouter along. Unfortunately my pack was back at the water's edge so I had to scramble down to it, keeping Meg in front of me. The going was much easier without the rucksack to encumber me. When I reached it, I put it on, lifted the dog and waded up to my waist along the final section of the water. I staggered onto the beach at the far side of the lochan like a shipwrecked sailor.

Making my way up to the head of the glen I scrambled over giant moss covered rocks interspersed with birch trees, still expecting to see a dinosaur at any moment. From the bealach the ground levelled out for a little before descending towards Loch Morar my destination. First I had to cross the river, which was coming down in a torrent from the big hills on the south side of the glen. Catching it as far upstream as was reasonably practical it was still too fast and deep for the dog. I went over with my rucksack first, using my walking poles to help balance then I dropped the rucksack and went back to carry Meg over, this time using just one pole to help balance.

Thankfully that was my difficulties over for the day. The descent was gentle and I soon picked up the path that took me down Gleann an Obain Bhig towards Loch Morar and Oban bothy. I was absolutely drenched and emotionally and physically drained after the trials and tribulations of just one day in rough terrain. I hoped and prayed to see a column of smoke as I neared the bothy. A fire was essential to dry out my clothes as well as my tent and my sleeping bag, which were soaking from the previous night. I really needed to talk to someone as well about my strenuous day.

Oblivious to my surroundings, I plodded along past Lochan an Obain Bhig and alongside Loch Morar, looking into the sky for grey wisps. Of smoke there was no trace but the bothy was a handsome whitewashed cottage and a godsend none the less. There was no one about but more importantly there was a small supply of firewood. I started a fire and got changed, hanging up all the wet gear that virtually filled the room. I now took stock. My nerves were jangling still. Today I had travelled only 18km but it felt like ten times that amount. I couldn't survive in the wilds at this rate. I still had almost six weeks to go. One afternoon of it and I was a wreck, my gear sodden and had it not been for me having the shelter of a bothy, I could barely have coped. Tomorrow's route was even more difficult, with few paths and finding my own way through the glens and over the hills. With more rain and mist it could be disastrous. I made a detailed hour-by-hour route plan in case the weather was poor and I couldn't see my surroundings. This exercise made me feel a little better so I cooked my dinner and then had a look at Meg's sores that were oozing puss. Damn.

Oban Bothy was similar to Glen Pean with two rooms downstairs and an upstairs sleeping area. No other hikers arrived in the evening so I had the place to myself. My fragile state of mind was demonstrated at bedtime. I started off sleeping upstairs, and then I thought I would be better off downstairs beside the fire. Lying downstairs I worried about Carbon Monoxide poisoning. Then I heard noises, little scratchings and feared what they might be coming from. I went back upstairs, now totally exhausted, but still I didn't sleep. I lay thinking about what I had been through, concerned about what difficulties tomorrow might hold in store.

Bonnie Prince Charlie had also rested in this vicinity after his first walk on foot. He had set out from the end of Loch Arkaig at five in the afternoon just a few hours later than me. His companion O'Sullivan called it the cruellest road. He was bloody right!

The following morning started off dry but misty. There were no views along Loch Morar and the surrounding mountains gave me palpitations. My plan was to reach the sea loch near Arisaig, where Bonnie Prince Charlie sailed over to Benbecula, one of the Western Isles. There were 21 mainly pathless kilometres in front of me before I would reach the shores of Loch nan Uamh. I was still wired as I left the bothy; my emotions in turmoil from the previous day. I followed a footpath along the loch, which I left behind to continue west and cross the river flowing down Glen Taodhail. On close inspection, it was flowing too fast to cross, forcing me to walk upstream for another twenty minutes before the waters eased off sufficiently. Even then I had to cross it three times. Once with my pack, back again unencumbered, and finally, over with Meg. Feet and boots soaking before 10am.

I found a faint stalkers path taking me uphill and round the craggy North East shoulder of Meith Bheinn, the dominant hill in the vicinity. This took me up to a pass at a height of 400m and from there I descended soggy ground into Coire Slaite and then onto a path by the river of the same name down to Meoble. So far so good, nerves stabilising. Dog looking good too.

Meoble is a shooting estate hemmed in by mountains and lochs, with just a tiny cluster of houses and no tarmac connection with the outside world. The vehicles on the estate have arrived by landing craft on Loch Morar. The soft green fields and mixed trees were a pleasant change from the brown of the heather-clad, rock-strewn hillsides of the morning. I chatted to an estate worker determined to take every opportunity to converse with people. I never knew how long it would

Meoble

be before I got the chance to talk to someone again and I figured that any local knowledge would be helpful, although to be fair, any which I had been given so far I had ignored to my detriment. Although the man was friendly he was unable to offer any advice about reaching Glen Beasdale.

After just a ten-minute lunch of various snacks I pushed on while the weather was dry, crossing the River Meoble and heading into a massive corrie with a wide flat, wet floor. I ascended alongside the waters of Abhainn Chlachach and then followed the Bhlair Dheirg stream that took me up to 250m, although it felt like a lot more on the pathless ground. From the plateau I walked south to two small lochans, the weather still holding up. My nerves were just about back to normal; I had made good progress, the good weather and easier going making all the difference. I headed now for the Bealach a Mhama the pass that connected the plateau with Glen Beasdale. Reaching the top of the pass, I was rewarded with breathtaking views to the coast, Loch nan Uamh (Loch of the Caves), the sound of Arisaig and the islands of the Western Seaboard. When Charles arrived here he must have felt a sense of achievement that he had come this far and that his brief stint of stravaiging was coming to an end. From here he could find a ship to take him back to France to lick his wounds.

Losing the path I descended steeply but very slowly into the deserted glen. Drum Fiaclach, a high craggy ridge with steep tree filled slopes adding some colour to the glen, formed the southern valley wall. Once down by the Beasdale Burn it was a pleasant jaunt down to the main road, the A830. Never had I been so pleased to see a road, I had made it. The first stage of my trip was almost complete. Just over two days ago I had been delighted to leave the public highway, now I welcomed it back like an old friend.

The euphoria soon wore off and I trauchled along the final kilometres to Borrodale House, rebuilt in the 18th century from the smoking ruins of a previous incarnation and now a large holiday cottage with swaying palm trees outside and an outstanding view over a little bay in Loch nan Uamh. In 1745 Bonnie Prince Charlie stayed at the previous version, prior to raising his standard at Glenfinnan. I carried on to nearby Arisaig House, an atmospheric Victorian building that has previously been an exclusive hotel and a private home but now is a welcoming family guesthouse. I was treated to coffee, questions and congratulations, whilst I broke into my bag of provisions that

Borrodale House

were stored in the laundry room. There was no room at the inn and I was glad, the temptation for a warm dry bed would have been overwhelming. I wanted to inspect the Prince's cave down by the bay. The proprietor, Sarah invited me up to the house for breakfast the following morning, which I accepted, hardly before the words had left her mouth.

Located amongst crags and rocks 100m back from the beach, the entrance to the cave was easily found. Going in feet first I descended one metre to an outer area and then crept through to an inner section. This sloped down towards the rear of the cave, which was a narrow channel approximately one metre wide tapering in as it rose to a height of two metres. The length of the cave was around three metres and the interior was damp and dank. Any thoughts of sleeping here were quickly dispelled; the floor of the cave was running with water.

It was a lovely evening and I camped by the beautiful beach in this glorious little bay. I was totally exhausted, but delighted that despite some misadventures, I had made it to the coast and completed the first stage of my journey.

Charles stayed in this area for a few days hoping to find a ship

Borrodale Bay Cave entrance

that would take him to France. But with no such ships in the area he decided to head for the Western Isles. Before departing he wrote a letter to the chiefs explaining that he could do little for them in Scotland and that he would best serve their interests by pleading directly with the King of France for assistance.

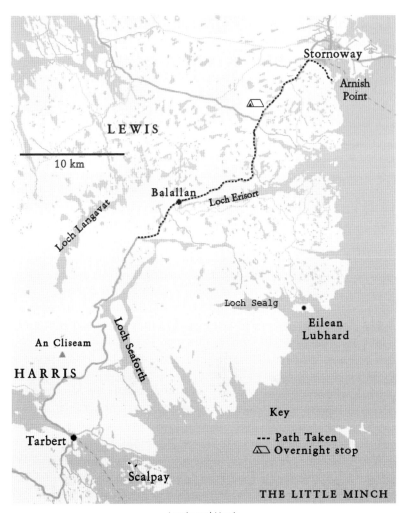

Lewis and Harris

CHAPTER 3

The Western Isles

THE FOLLOWING MORNING I was in the kitchen of Arisaig House sitting at a farmhouse table with a cup of freshly brewed coffee in hand.

Watching others rush around as they prepared breakfast for the guests was very relaxing. An order came through from the dining room for scrambled egg and mushrooms with the fat removed. This caused some discussion in the kitchen between the chef and the boss on the best way to achieve this nigh impossible request. The end result was 'make it like it you normally would,' which amused me greatly.

After the last seven days, watching someone else prepare my breakfast was a sight to savour. When it was put in front of me I wolfed it down, partly because it was tasty and partly because I was going to be late for my train to Mallaig. Miss that and the next train wasn't for another four hours and the local buses didn't allow dogs on board. Yomping uphill to Beasdale station fully laden and with a full stomach, I arrived with a couple of moments to spare, layered in sweat and lucky not to have done myself an injury with my heavy rucksack bouncing all over the place.

Charles had sailed from Loch nan Uamh across the Minch to the Rosinish peninsula on Benbecula. Without chartering a boat myself, the most direct way for me to travel to the Western Isles was via the Isle of Skye. The first stage of my journey would be a rail trip from Beasdale station to the port of Mallaig where I could catch a ferry for Skye. This would be a short trip on a small part of the West Highland Line, a 67km stretch between Fort William and Mallaig, which is one of the best railway journeys in the world. The steam train that runs the line attracts more tourists than you could shake a wand at. Starting under the shadow of Ben Nevis, the loch side and mountain scenery is stunningly beautiful as the route progresses towards the coast; the most famous highlight of course is crossing the Glenfinnan viaduct featured in the Harry Potter films.

Today the beautiful blue skies made even my small section of the route extra special and the comforting clickety-clack of the wheels on the tracks reminded me that someone else was doing all the work. The views from the train were stunning; little boats dotted in Arisaig harbour, the white sands of Morar and the familiar shapes of the Isles of Rhum and Eigg, the 'cocktail isles.' In the distance, the Isle of Skye with its distinctive peaks shaped like an upturned saw blade. With a sprint finish, we raced cars travelling along the newly upgraded home straight.

Both fishing boats and ferry traffic use the busy port of Mallaig. As well as travelling to Skye or the Small Isles on the large, well-equipped Caledonian MacBrayne Ferries, you can also take a smaller independently owned ferry over to Inverie on the Knoydart Peninsula, Britain's last wilderness and a place inaccessible by car.

After buying my ferry ticket, I went to seek out a vet to look at Meg's sores. I knew that a specialist visited on a Wednesday. At the community centre I found it was only every second week that a vet was available. Bah! Wandering round the village I found a chemist shop, but I couldn't convince the pharmacist to examine Meg. She did however, give me a bold and vivid description of what infected sores looked like. Bright red, inflamed, bulging, seeping pus. I could see one or two of the customers going green at the thought. I inspected Meg on the pavement outside in case I needed further advice but her sores although tender looking didn't fit the lurid description. By the time I had applied half a tube of antiseptic cream you could hardly see them.

I wandered round a couple more shops and although it was a little early for them to be bustling or brisk, there were people about and the tills were ringing. It felt good just to be amongst people, hearing everyday sounds, saying hello to those walking by, listening to snippets of conversation. Taking a seat by the harbour and watching the world go by was the perfect tonic after six days of continuous walking. My attention was drawn to a huddle of men talking and gesticulating on the pier. They brought to mind the parliament of St Kilda where the men of the island met in the village street to discuss the day's work and how it would be shared out. The archipelago of St Kilda lies 64km west of the Western Isles and was inhabited until 1930 by people surviving on the multitudes of seabirds that made their nests on the sea cliffs, the highest in Britain.

A rumour that the Prince had gone to St Kilda sent ships from the

British Navy scurrying to these islands. The isolated inhabitants probably wondered what hit them when the vessels arrived. They had never heard of the monarch at the time, George II, never mind Bonnie Prince Charlie. All they had heard was that their MacLeod chief had done battle with a lady in Europe and he had won.

Although news into the islands was dependent on passing boats, the people did have a method of communicating with the outside world called the St Kilda mail boat. During the winter when the weather prevented launching their own boats, islanders would put a message in a wooden vessel tied to an inflated sheep's stomach, which acted as a float. This was launched into the ocean and the islanders knew the tides and winds well enough to hurl it into the water at the appropriate time to ensure that the package would be washed ashore on Harris in the Western Isles within a matter of days. The mail boat saved the islanders from starvation on more than one occasion.

Tourists now launch 'novelty mail boats' containing postcards. Some are never seen again but quite often they are carried by the North Atlantic Drift and have been known to turn up in Orkney, Shetland or even as far afield as Norway.

Daydreams of St Kilda were brought to a sudden halt when Nicola, her friend Carol and the kids surprised me with a visit. They were all still on holiday in the area and having great fun without me, it seemed. Although it had only been a few days since I had seen them, it felt like much longer. Already the kids had loads to tell me, all at once of course! I was treated to lunch in The Tea Garden before I boarded the ferry.

Just a short hop over to Skye on the Calmac Ferry. I sat out at the bow with Meg. Together we faced the bracing wind, waving farewell. Once again I was on my own...

On this occasion Skye was just a stepping-stone to the Western Isles but it became a major part of the Prince's escape route. Near to the pier where we disembarked was the Clan Donald Centre and Museum of the Isles, situated in the gardens of Armadale Castle. Historically, this southern tip of Skye belonged to the MacDonalds of Sleat a branch of Clan Donald. Charles was sorely disappointed in 1745 when the 7th Baronet refused to join the rising. This was despite having made previous assurances that the clan would rise. However

MacDonald had had to buy his family's estates back after they were confiscated following the previous rising in 1715 and probably gauged that, without French assistance, Charles' chances of success were too slim to risk the estates once again.

A local bus service operates infrequently from the pier but I had timed my ferry to meet it. My plan was to travel to Portree, the island's largest town, and from there journey onwards to Uig, to catch a ferry to the Western Isles. However, instead of Portree, the bus now went only as far as Broadford, some 30km short of where I needed to be. The only connection between Portree and Broadford would be on a Citylink bus that wouldn't allow dogs. It wasn't my fault that the schedule had changed without notice, so I decided to plead a special case to the Citylink driver, and see if he would allow me to travel. Short of walking or getting a taxi, there was no alternative. I was booked into a bed and breakfast in Uig and neither hell nor high water was preventing me from sleeping soundly on a sprung mattress that night. I had plenty of time to think about my plea because the Citylink bus wasn't due for another hour and a half. Broadford is the second largest town on the island and is on the main road linking the Skye Bridge with Portree. There were shops and attractions to explore but I ended up passing the time with another couple of travellers, a teacher from South Africa now based in England, and a man from Finland. We found plenty to talk about and when I was explaining that I felt a little daunted by what lay in front of me, the teacher made a great point. Asking me what my longest hill-walking trip was previously, I answered 'one week.'

'Well look at it this way, you have already matched your longest ever trip, everything else is a new record.' I felt so much better after that.

The Citylink bus duly arrived and as expected, the driver explained the no-dog policy to me, pointing out he could lose his job for breaking the rules. Nevertheless once I explained my predicament he allowed me on board. As luck would have it this bus was in fact going onwards to Uig after Portree, so I wouldn't have to change.

I was in Skye on the 130th anniversary of the Battle of the Braes that took place south of Portree. The local crofters had forced the burning of eviction notices, which their landlord had served on them after they reclaimed previously removed grazing rights for their cattle. The Sheriff of Inverness set off with 50 Glasgow policemen to arrest the ringleaders. Having made the arrests and returning to Portree the sheriff and his constables were met by around 100 crofters armed with rocks and stones. The ensuing fracas as the police attempted to break through the crowd was witnessed by reporters and brought a national spotlight to the crofters' plight.

Political pressure forced the government to set up a Royal Commission to look at crofters' grievances which eventually led to the Crofters Act of 1886 which gave a more secure way of life to Scotland's crofting community. After more than one hundred years of mistreatment, the people of the Highlands and Islands had won a major victory against oppressive landlords and an unsympathetic and distant government.

I stayed at the Uig Bay campsite, where I was in the relative luxury of a little self-contained apartment, which gave me use of a kitchen/living area. Working like a Trojan I unpacked, sorted, dried out and reorganised all my gear. The Atlantic winds were blowing what locals called a good breeze, and I nearly broke my ankles on the rocky beach, chasing my tent along the shore after it had blown off the line. The bloody thing was nearly in the Western Isles before me. The little luxuries of my stay were all very welcome. Using a proper cooker to heat my dinner, sitting comfortably watching a bit of TV at night, lying in a bed and being able to stretch out without touching wet nylon all felt tremendous and I awoke duly refreshed, although my body seemed stiff as if the weeks camping had caught up with it. Beefed up by a second gigantic cooked breakfast in as many days, I was ready once more to hit the trail. Within a few minutes of leaving the B&B, I was on the ferry and bound for Tarbert, on Harris. It was another beautiful day as we sailed away. Looking over to the Waternish Peninsula, high cliffs rose from the sea with a single line of houses resting atop them. Behind the white dotted homes were rolling hills and a layer of curly cumulus clouds that eventually gave way to bright blue sky.

Charlie's journey to the Western Isles was very nearly his last. He, who knew little, convinced the Highlanders who knew a lot, to set out on their journey. A party of eight oarsmen, Donald MacLeod the pilot, and the Prince's companions set sail in what quickly turned out to be a major storm. The Prince was soon for turning back saying he would rather face cannons and muskets than this storm. However the helmsman knew that to do so would run the risk of being dashed against the rocks of Loch nan Uamh, so he made for open seas. On 27 April 1746, the Prince's boat was driven by the raging storm to Rosinish on Benbecula. Despite severe sea sickness the Prince had remained calm during the horrendous voyage, where at times those aboard must have thought their last moments had come. They arrived on land soaked to the skin and occupied a small hut by the shore where Charles was visited by the local chief, Clanranald who lived on the other side of the island.

This Chief's son had come out for the Jacobites and a regiment of Clanranald MacDonalds had fought at all the major engagements in 1745 and 1746. Charles was determined to find passage to France, so two days later he sailed onwards and landed on the Isle of Scalpay on his way to Stornoway. During his two-month spell in the Western Isles, Charles plied up and down the coast as he attempted to evade capture. Practicality prevented me from retracing his every route, but I would replicate the major land journeys that he undertook on these islands and visit as many of his numerous landing places as possible. I was going to pick up the Prince's route from Scalpay, only a short distance from my own landing place at Tarbert. I would visit the Rosinish peninsula at a later date.

As I sailed down Loch Tarbert I saw hilly landscapes ahead, where houses were clinging to the shore. There were heather clad slopes and lots of exposed grey rock. A splattering of small islands surrounded me, the largest of which, Scalpay was on the starboard side. The sleek bridge connecting it to Harris looked futuristic in this otherwise very natural setting. The village of Tarbert is on a narrow strip of land that connects north and south Harris. I had hoped to be greeted with brightly painted houses like the neat little harbours at Portree or Tobermory but the more chaotic mix of buildings and their everyday paint jobs were not as attractive to the eye. My shallow thoughts however were soon put into perspective as shortly afterwards I had a simple experience that was one of the highlights of my whole trip.

Leaving the ferry I left my bags at the tourist office, and I jumped on a small local bus for Scalpay. The driver wasn't on the bus yet, although one or two passengers were. Ceilidh music was playing quietly in the background. By the time the driver embarked the little bus was nearly full. Those in front of me handed their bus passes to the driver, who glanced at them and returned them. He then gave me a look. 'What about you?' Everyone in front turned to look at me. I was in the spotlight. I wanted to buy a ticket to travel around all of the Western Isles, a sort of day-tripper card. The bus being too small to get up and down with others on board, I shouted forward my requests. After a public discussion with the driver it was soon established that this wasn't going to be possible, so I asked for a single ticket and passed forward my money to the person in front who passed it forward until it reached the driver. He looked out the change due and passed it back in the same fashion. Conversations between the driver and others behind me then took place in Gaelic and we were on our way.

The first thing the driver did was to turn the music up, loud! This started the party. Suddenly everyone was talking to one another in Gaelic. Sounds of laughter added to the atmosphere. The music played to my emotions as the bus bounced along the narrow hilly roads. Suddenly overcome, I had to bite my lip to stop myself shouting 'Eeeeeeuch.' If the aisles had been wider I would've done a 'pas-de-basque' and I don't think I'd have been the only one either.

Scalpay is a small island, now connected to Harris by a modern single-track bridge. It has a population of around 400. The main settlement is clustered round North Harbour, and I got off the bus in the centre of the village, my fellow passengers having directed me to the old parish manse. This 19th century home was built on the site of an earlier house where Bonnie Prince Charlie had stayed for a few days. Originally, a stone tablet above the door had a Gaelic inscription, which translated as, 'On this site was the house in which Prince Charles spent part of his days as a wandering exile in his own rightful kingdom.' Unfortunately a new wing has been added to the house covering over the original doorway. However, a marble plate has been affixed bearing a copy of the original inscription engraved in both Gaelic and English. The original building has been converted to a three storey, L-shaped house and further exterior works were underway when I arrived.

Knocking on the door I was greeted by a man in a facemask. Undeterred I introduced myself and Mr Haye explained he was busy

AIR AN LARACH SEO BHA AN TIGH ANNS DO CHUIR
AM PRIONNSA TEARLACH SEACHAD CUID
DE LAITHEAN ALLABANACH MAR FHOGARRACH
NA DHUTHAICH DHLIGHICH FHEIN.

ON THIS SITE WAS THE HOUSE IN WHICH
BONNIE PRINCE CHARLIE PASSED SOME OF HIS
DAYS AS A FUGITIVE IN HIS
OWN RIGHTFUL LAND.

Inscription at Scalpay

sandblasting. His wife joined him at the doorway and they told me they had recently purchased the house and were busy converting it into a Bed & Breakfast. When I explained the purpose of my visit they weren't in the least surprised. 'We often get mad people here on the trail of Bonnie Prince Charlie' Mr Haye said, quickly following it up with 'Not that I'm saying you are mad or anything.'

Taking a great interest in my journey they invited me in, and showed me some of the original features of the house including an eye-catching fireplace with a gigantic stone lintel. A real fireplace is often my favourite feature in a house and this one was stunning. Sitting round a roaring fire always brings me a primordial calmness, basking in a glow which stretches back thousands of years to caveman ancestors.

The back of the house looks over Acarasiadh a Tuath, the North Harbour an excellent sheltered bay. Amazing to think that the Prince's boat may have been pulled up on the very shingle at the foot of the house.

On arrival here, Charles was shown hospitality by Donald Campbell in whose house he remained whilst Donald MacLeod, the Prince's pilot went on to Stornoway. When MacLeod returned after four days, having managed to charter a ship, the Prince's party resumed their journey north and sailed into Loch Seaforth, where Charles alighted at the head of the Loch to complete his journey on foot.

I walked along the road following the natural harbour to another pier at the entrance to the bay before realising I was going to be late for public transport once more. I ran back to the centre of the village where sheep and lambs were wandering freely around the streets. The bus arrived almost immediately but when I went to step on the bus, the same driver pointed to a sign 'No Dogs.' I was dumbstruck.

'What?' I stammered.

'I shouldn't have let you on earlier. There's a lady with asthma uses this bus. But it's okay, jump on. Seeing that I brought you here, I'll take you back. I don't think she'll be on today anyway.'

'Phew!'

I chatted to the driver on the way back to Tarbert, adopting my nervous idiom of asking stupid questions. However once we got on to the price of fuel I was on safe ground and we took turns ranting and raving about penalties that it brings to life in remote communities. I asked about whether the price of fuel had reduced noticeably since the introduction of the fuel duty discount scheme for the Western Isles. That was another stupid question.

Next I boarded a bus heading for Stornoway where the driver agreed to make a special stop for me at the head of Loch Seaforth. We headed north, pausing only to pick up a parcel on the edge of the village where the driver was scolded by the impatient parcel-giver for being five minutes late. I chided him 'you get away with nothing here.' Unless the parcel was something vital such as a kidney, the retort of 'Deliver your own bloody parcel the next time' would have been a perfectly reasonable riposte

The driver bothered not one jot. It was probably me that had made him late anyway, the rigmarole of boarding a bus whilst trying to manoeuvre a huge rucksack past people on narrow aisles without smacking them in the face, my walking sticks in one hand and holding on to Meg with my other. Then getting off the bus again to collect bags of newly purchased provisions.

There were five minutes to be made up as we whizzed through the rugged hills of northern Harris. The highest mountain in the whole of the Western Isles, An Clisham (799m) was ahead as the road approached Loch Seaforth.

Charles sailed up this 22km loch on his way to Stornoway and the bus driver dropped me at its head. A large teardrop-shaped memorial cairn marks the spot where Charles landed. The shape of the cairn represents tears of frustration on behalf of the participants in the Rising, and the tears of the people after the Rising when they were brutally suppressed. It was designed and built by local stonemason James Crawford whose ancestor died at Culloden. The cairn is at a beautiful vantage point and marked the starting point of my walk.

Memorial at Loch Seaforth

The territory ahead belonged to Lewis. Harris and Lewis are two territories on the same island. The border is an invisible east/west line that runs between Loch Resort and Loch Seaforth. Where Harris is hilly, Lewis is low lying. Lewis has a population of over 18,000 people whereas Harris has a population of approximately 2,000 people. The overall size of the island is 2,178 square kilometres, of which approximately 80 per cent belongs to Lewis. The plateau in front of me was peat-covered moorland, filled with hundreds of lochs and lochans. In this territory the Prince's party got hopelessly lost, and it would be a miserable bunch floundering through the peat bogs that finally made it to Kildun House, just south of Stornoway. I had the luxury of the A859, which follows the approximate route that the Prince should have travelled. The road was quiet and the majority of the traffic that did pass made allowances for Meg and I.

The first settlement I came to was Balallan which was home to some of the Deer Park Raiders of 1887, to whom a large memorial was dedicated just off the main road. When the proprietor of Lewis turned a sheep farm into a sporting estate, a group of men set out to reclaim the ground that their forebears had been evicted from in order to make the sheep farm. The protesters wished to highlight the plight of the oppressed crofters. The government responded by sending in the army and arresting the ringleaders but the following year, in a blaze of publicity, they were acquitted of all charges. The raiders had succeeded in highlighting their poverty with the government shown to be heavy handed in its response to what essentially was a cry for help.

The afternoon turned dry and bright while the north wind blew strongly into my face. Quite a few of the homes by the roadside still had old black houses within their gardens, some in ruins, some still in use as garden sheds. Local people lived with a constant reminder of their ancestors and thus a greater awareness of their past than people in other parts of the country. I continued on the road for the rest of the day and into early evening, disappointed that there were no shops or cafés where I could escape the wind and break up my journey a little. (There were a couple of art galleries but I couldn't pretend to be interested in buying any pictures, nor could I have carried them.) By the time I passed a garage/shop at Leurbost it had closed for the evening.

The road continued along the east side of Lewis so I didn't get the opportunity to see Callanish Standing Stones or Carloway Broch. Visiting these fantastic remains would, in normal circumstances, have been top of my to-do list, but no matter how many books I read, nobody ever placed Charles at either of these sites. By 8pm, a combination of tiredness and the biting cold wind forced me off the road. I was only just over a week into my walk and I was still paranoid about getting hypothermia.

I camped by Loch a Chnoic Dubhe and came across traps with hooded crows inside. I wondered why there was a need to catch crows, but subsequently found out that they are a menace to sheep when they are lambing, pecking out the eyes of ewes while they give birth, or even the eyes of the newly born lambs. The following morning having left our rucksacks hidden by the main road, Meg and I headed along an unclassified road towards Arnish Point. Unencumbered, we moved at the speed of a couple of Exocet missiles. At the end of the road on a small heathery hilltop was a giant commemorative cairn to the Prince. Climbing alongside this memorial there were good views over Stornoway bay to the town, Lews Castle and the striking Lewis War Memorial.

When Charles arrived here a Mrs Mackenzie gave him shelter in Kildun House. Unfortunately there is no trace of the house anymore. Donald MacLeod returned, and told him not to enter Stornoway, as the local

Arnish Point

people had got wind of his arrival and were fearful of government retribution should they allow him into the town. An armed band of Mackenzies had formed to prevent the Prince from entering. He had no option but to abandon his plans and from here he set sail in a small boat eastwards towards the mainland. British warships were now patrolling the sea between, the Minch, and the little party were thus obliged to about turn or risk capture. They stopped at the tiny Isle of Iubhard, remaining there for four days. Once again they travelled on to Scalpay, where their host was now in hiding from the government forces, so they sailed on to Loch Uskavagh on Benbecula, narrowly avoiding more British patrol boats on the way.

Unlike the Prince, I went into Stornoway where I intended to catch a bus to get to Benbecula. I just couldn't squeeze in a visit to Isle of Iubhard, having missed the only bus that would have allowed me to keep to my timetable. So I consoled myself with the fact that there was little to see on the uninhabited island and no walking to be done on the Isle.

Before making their contribution to the new world, Scots tried to colonise the more unruly parts of their own realm including Lewis. In 1598 a group called the Fife Adventurers, with the permission of King James vi founded a settlement at Stornoway to try to exploit the

Stornoway Harbour

resources from the island. Understandably the local MacLeods did not take well to this invasion and eventually the incomers were repulsed.

On my way into Stornoway I passed the entrance to Lews castle and I should have taken a shortcut through the grounds to reach the town itself but I was hurrying along and hadn't consulted my map properly so I missed the chance to see the castle and grounds close up. Even from a distance the building was impressive. A 19th century castellated mansion, it was built by Sir James Matheson with profits he had made from the opium trade in China.

With a population of over 9,000 people, Stornoway is the major town and administrative centre of the Western Isles. With an airport, ferry links to the mainland and a decent local bus service it's as well connected as it could possibly be. There were plenty of shops for me to buy supplies with a decent mix of national and local names above the doors.

I boarded a bus bound for Leverburgh on the southwest coast of Harris, the first stage of my journey to Benbecula, as I tried to catch up with the Prince. Battering along the road was exhilarating and yet dispiriting at the same time. I had spent the previous 24 hours walking 33kms to reach Stornoway via Arnish point, and there I was arriving back in Tarbert in less than an hour.

The prince must have been much more upset than me. His plans were now in tatters as he sailed away, and he had no strategy now for removing himself from Scotland. He would have to depend on others to shelter him whilst he hoped for French assistance.

At Tarbert, I switched to a smaller and more crowded bus. Initially we weaved our way through hilly ground until we reached Harris's west coast and its long, glorious and undisturbed sandy beaches. This stretch of beauty, in its own way, matches all the mountains and lochs for which the Highlands and Islands are rightly famed.

It was straight off the bus and onto the ferry, which left right away. This sailing was taking me from Harris to the Uists, a group of islands including Berneray, North Uist, Benbecula, South Uist and Eriskay, connected to one another by causeways. Crossing the Sound of Harris was immense. Bright sunshine was sparkling on the sea and I was sailing through a beautiful seascape of 100 tiny islands. Meg was popular with the school children on board and one of the teachers recommended a campsite for the evening. Disembarking on Berneray I was straight onto another bus for Benbecula. This was a proper joined up public transport system.

It was bright and sunny; one of those days where it wouldn't take you long to dry your washing. The sea was travel brochure blue and seals were basking on the rocks near the small settlement of Borgh. Lucky black Hebridean lambs were skipping around. Lucky because the lambs of this breed are too skinny to be sold for their meat, so they live a longer life. As we crossed the causeway to go to North Uist there was an official Department of Transport warning sign to watch out for otters crossing. Hooray! The bus driver was very friendly and gave me a running commentary on the local sights. The people talk so beautifully there, you could listen all day.

North Uist is a land of freshwater lochs, and features Scotland's oldest Crannog, an artificial island settlement built on a loch that affords protection and status to its occupiers. At Loch Olabhat, the crannog remains are over 5,500 years old. Today's population of 1,300 people are mostly settled on the machair; a fertile, low lying, grass covered sand located on the west coast of the island. Rich in plant life, it can surprise in spring and summer with a riot of colour. Contrarily, the main settlement, Lochmaddy, being a ferry port, is on the east coast. Here we swapped buses and continued on our journey.

The bus left North Uist on an eight-kilometre causeway that connects with Benbecula via the western tip of the Isle of Grimsay. With a population of around 200 people, the island has a significant shellfish industry centred on the harbour at the hamlet of Kallin. This was no guided tour however and the bus continued into Benbecula.

Benbecula is very flat with fertile ground and beautiful sandy beaches on the west. The eastern side is peat moorland with a rocky coastline incorporating many small islands and inlets. The interior is filled with small, interconnected lochans. Like North Uist the population of approximately 1,200 is based on the west coast.

It was to the rocky eastern coast that the Prince was initially washed up on his arrival in the Western Isles and to the east coast that he landed again after his unsuccessful journey to Stornoway.

The bus journeyed down the more populous west coast road, past the airport. I jumped off a few kilometres further along the road at Lionaclet where I headed for the campsite to take advantage of shower facilities. Later, I walked to nearby Griminish following tracks and paths through the level ground for a meeting of the Islands Book Trust. Arriving at St Marys Church, I saw a door ajar between the priest's house and the church, and thinking this may be the meeting place I went inside. As soon as I stepped in, the priest came out of his house to catch me red handed in his storage cupboard. If I'd been in a city the incumbent would've belted me thinking I was nicking his bike.

Finding the correct hall at an entirely separate building nearby, I met with Alasdair MacEachen. The aim of the Islands Book Trust is to further understand the history of Scottish Islands as well as to generate economic, social and cultural benefit for island communities. There was to be a talk, slideshow and film about the island of Wiay, which along with some members of the group I was planning to visit the following day.

Alasdair's great grandfather, Calum MacRae, had been the last resident tenant on this now uninhabited island, the largest off the east coast of Benbecula. One or two other members of the group were also related to this father of ten children. My interest was that Bonnie Prince Charlie had stayed on the island on two occasions, and I was looking forward to seeing the cave where Charles had hidden.

It turned out that the Prince wasn't the only famous escapee to

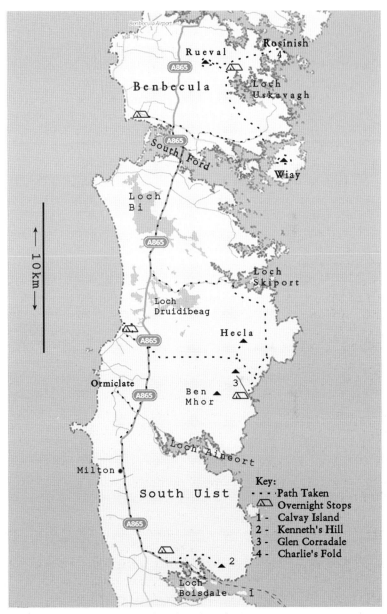

Benbecula and South Uist

have hidden on the island. The celebrity bear, Hercules, who used to wrestle with his owner Andy Robin on national television, escaped in 1980 and swam over to Wiay. Despite extensive searches he was not found. Then, after nearly four weeks, he was spotted on North Uist by a local crofter and recaptured, further increasing his fame.

I was given the opportunity to explain my mission to the group and at the end of the night many people came forward to wish me well. As usual, people spoke to Meg more than to me!

The following morning a party of 12 sailed out from Petersport over to Wiay, skippered by Duncan MacRae, another of Calum's descendants. It was a bright day as we crossed the channel and pulled up against some slippery rocks. To get ashore, one lithe member of our party jumped onto the rocks and pulled the boat in. The rest of us climbed out and onto the seaweed covered stones as best we could. In poor weather this manoeuvre must be treacherous. We stopped to examine the old croft house, frozen in time and surrounded by tough wild irises. All the walls remain intact even although it was abandoned in 1942. Ten children were brought up in this two-room house.

Arriving on Wiay

To the east of the island, at the foot of Beinn a Tuath, is Prince Charlie's Rest. Formed by a tumble of large rocks at the foot of some cliffs and hidden amongst heather, the diamond shaped entrance is only 50cm wide and decorated with dog violets, a welcome splash of purple.

I lowered myself feet first into the darkness and then squeezed the rest of my body through the narrow aperture. Crouching, I crawled through an inner entrance on hands and knees. The main chamber is eight feet long, high enough to sit up in and about four feet wide. A chink of light gave some illumination to the cave.

Neither Meg nor any other member of the party ventured in. This cave felt comfortable for me on my own, but for the Prince, sitting round a fire with a couple of companions, it must have been claustrophobic.

Standing at the entrance to this remote and well hidden hiding place, the Prince would have clear views up and down the Minch and over to the Isle of Skye. He would have felt reasonably secure as he watched British Navy warships as they patrolled up and down, combing the seas for him.

Cave entrance on Wiay

Climbing the hill behind the cave I could survey the flat terrain of Benbecula and look further on to the hills of the surrounding islands.

Whilst at the Co-op store first thing that morning, I had struggled to get any oatcakes for my packed lunch. Oatcakes were a vital part of my own diet with meat paste, peanut butter or dried fruit the usual supplements. During our stop for lunch I noticed quite a few of the islanders had oatcakes too, much as their forebears would have had.

During Charles' time, oats were replacing barley as the staple cereal crop in the Highlands. It was a hardy crop and provided more nutrition than barley. By necessity the Prince was a big fan, and liked his oatcakes well fired and flavoured. Whatever was available would be mixed in for taste; on one occasion it was cows' brains.

But if time was short to make oatcakes, then brose was a speedy alternative: simply pour boiling water over oats and eat as soon as practicable. As well as being quicker to make, it also avoided the shrinkage that resulted from cooking porridge. Whilst at sea Charles mixed oats with cold salt water to make dramach, but he never complained of the fare. As Donald MacLeod said of the Prince,

> Never any meat or drink came wrong to him, for he could take a share of everything be it good bad or indifferent, and was always cheerful and contented in every condition.

Back on the boat we sailed round the island for a bit and I was shown a couple of eagle nests. Once back at Petersport, Deirdre MacEachen offered to take me down to Loch Boisdale in South Uist where Charles headed to gain shelter and support from MacDonald of Boisdale.

Deirdre works with Stòras Uibhist, landlord of the South Uist Estate, a community group that manages 93,000 acres of land covering nearly the whole of the islands of Benbecula, South Uist and Eriskay.

This has been the largest community land purchase in Scotland and one of the first major projects has been the building of a 6.9 Megawatt wind farm at Loch Carnan. The turbines will generate enough electricity to power 20,000 homes. The revenues generated will be reinvested in the Islands.

We arrived at Lochboisdale, which is a small community with a row of whitewashed shops and offices overlooking the harbour and loch of the same name. The ferry link with Oban via the Isle of Barra is

South Uist's only sea borne link with Scottish mainland. This journey takes five hours and is infrequent. Local people would prefer a direct link to Mallaig, which would take less than three hours, and there's a good chance of this happening in the near future as Stòras Uibhist has recently secured the final tranche of £10 million of funding for the Lochboisdale Regeneration Project. This will allow the expansion of the harbour and pier facilities and involve the building of new roads and sites for housing, providing a massive economic boost for the area and providing a firm base for sustained economic growth.

Whilst Deirdre went to try to enlist the support of a local fisherman to take me out to Calvay Island, I had a wander along by the pier. Here I met a proponent of an activity I am very much a champion of, lazy-man's dog exercising. Whereas I would throw a ball in the park to exhaust my dogs, this shepherd had six border collies swimming across the harbour chasing after a ring. The barking and splashing provided a bit of atmosphere on an otherwise quiet afternoon. Meg nearly pulled me into the water, so desperate was she to join in.

With one of the local fishermen coaxed away from watching the Grand National on television, we set off for Calvay Island on a large dinghy, with Deirdre and two of her friends who came along for the hell of it.

Just as the Prince had done I was depending on a local family called MacEachen to help me complete my journey. In fact, both Deirdre and Alasdair are related to Neil MacEachen, the Prince's companion and guide on the Western Isles.

Educated in Paris, Neil was the tutor to the children of Clanranald. He kept Charles securely hidden and guided him safely across moors and mountains for a large proportion of the time that the Prince spent in Benbecula, South Uist and Skye.

After the Rising, Neil was forced into exile in France where he became an officer in the French Army. He lived latterly in some degree of poverty in Sancerre, where he died in 1788. Perhaps unfairly, he never achieved the same degree of fame that Flora MacDonald received for her exploits.

His son Alexander went on to become a key figure in French affairs of the early 19th century. Starting off as a Lieutenant, he rose to the rank of General within two years. Napoleon made him Marshal of

France and Duke of Tarentum in 1809. After Napoleon's abdication (which he helped to negotiate) Louis XVIII made him a minister of state.

Despite having been an enemy of the British as one of Napoleon's Generals, Marshall Macdonald returned to a hero's welcome in the Uists when he returned in 1825 to visit the land of his forefathers.

The wind was blowing towards us as the dinghy gingerly made its way out of the bay past the little island of Gasaigh. As the waters of Loch Boisdale opened out the boat bounced along on the incoming waves. Our pilot asked us if we wanted to go back for oilskins, I was going to say aye, but the girls thought we would manage. The further out of the bay we got, the bigger the waves and soon the boat was leaping high in the water, with the occasional dunt when we hit a trough. However the girls were proved right – thanks to our skilled pilot we remained relatively dry.

Reaching Calvay, a small inlet offered shelter and allowed us to tie the boat up easily and jump ashore. The weather looked like it was going to turn for the worse so we hurried along, over the heather and onto the little promontory on which the fort was built. This fort had guarded the entrance to the bay and would have provided early warning of approaching galleys. From a distance, the walls almost blended in with the rocky crags. Meg stood atop the remnants to survey the scene, looking every inch the queen of all that she surveyed.

Approaching Calvay Island

Fort remains on Calvay

Having sailed south from Benbecula, the Prince hid on this island, amongst the ruins, before heading for the shores of Loch Boisdale.

On the return journey, with the wind at our back, the boat sped over the waves at an exhilarating speed bringing us to the pier in half the time. I had a drink with my fellow sailors at the Lochboisdale Hotel whilst we watched the last furlong of the Grand National, before it was time to be back on my lonely way once again.

Charles had come to this area to seek shelter with MacDonald of Boisdale but MacDonald had been arrested. The Prince remained in the area for a few days, skulking by the shore, narrowly avoiding the large numbers of troops out looking for him. When government forces landed within a mile of his resting place, he was forced to move swiftly.

At this point, the Prince parted company from Donald MacLeod, Ned Burke and O'Sullivan, men that he would not have parted from had not the situation been so desperate. O'Neil, Neil MacEachen and the Prince retreated to the top of Beinn Ruigh Choinnich, a hill overlooking Loch Boisdale, and made their plans for escape.

Donald MacLeod was soon captured and taken before General Campbell. His loyalty to Charles was typical of that of Highlanders in general, who displayed a commitment to the Prince that in today's society we would find unimaginable.

A reward of £30,000 was offered by the government for capturing the Prince, which was a colossal sum in 1746. Given the pressure that Highlanders were under as their families were attacked, their homes burned and their cattle driven off, the fact that Charles was never turned in is a testimony to the loyalty of the people and the unwritten code of conduct by which they lived their lives.

This poster ridiculing the Prince was issued by the government and offered a £30,000 reward for his capture.

Donald's words are quoted directly from his narrative in the *Lyon in Mourning*:

What then? Thirty thousand pounds! Though I had gotten't I could not have enjoyed it eight and forty hours. Conscience would have gotten up upon me. That money could not have kept it down. And tho' I could have gotten all England and Scotland for my pains I would not have allowed a hair of his body to be touched if I could help it.

I headed out of the village and back along the A865 until I was able to cross the outflow of Loch a Bharp. Once over the concrete causeway I headed along the north shore of Loch Boisdale towards the hilltop of Beinn Ruigh Choinnich (Kenneth's Hill). A muddy track took me to the foot of the steep slopes before it eventually died away amongst the bracken and the heather. Nonetheless Meg and I made good time as we climbed steeply. At the 276m summit we were rewarded with clear views in all directions.

From this viewpoint the Prince's party could have made their desperate plans whilst keeping an eye on the movement of the government troops below. MacEachen led O'Neil and Charles to Ormiclate where they would seek help from a certain Flora MacDonald.

I made my way back to the main road and to the Lochside Bed and Breakfast. It was around 8pm when I arrived and Mr and Mrs MacDonald allowed me use of their kitchen to cook myself a meal.

Lochboisdale from Beinn Ruigh Choinnich

We chatted for a while, any unfamiliarity washed away by the warmth of their welcome.

The following morning, the sky was clear and a beautiful shade of blue. I sat in the conservatory that overlooked a small lochan, so close you could comfortably fish out of the window if you so desired.

Mr MacDonald served me a fabulous cooked breakfast, but first I had a massive bowl of porridge that was the best I have ever tasted. He let me into his wife's secret, 'soak the oats overnight.'

With another cracking day in store I headed north towards Ormiclate. It was Sunday morning and the road was quiet. Meg walked freely by the roadside, and I called her to me if traffic approached. Soon I reached Daliburgh where the road splits and can be followed over a causeway to the isle of Eriskay, the final island in the Uists chain.

The '45 has left a tangible historical backdrop to many highland locations and none more so than Eriskay where Charles first landed in Scotland with a just handful of supporters, to begin the Rising.

The sinking of the ss *Politician* in 1941 has given Eriskay equally comparable fame. The ship ran aground between Eriskay and South Uist and when Islanders found out that the cargo included 28,000 cases of whisky, a major illicit salvage operation was launched. Up to 24,000 cases were said to have been removed by men from as far afield as Lewis.

However, the local customs officer was determined that the looting should stop and that those responsible should be punished. One or two islanders were fined or spent a few weeks in a mainland prison, but the majority of the whisky was never recovered. The story was immortalised in the 1949 film 'Whisky Galore'.

Going straight on at the Daliburgh crossroads takes one to Hallan Cemetery. Located nearby are remains of Bronze and Iron Age settlements. What's believed to be the first evidence of mummification in ancient Britain was discovered at Cladh Hallan, buried underneath a prehistoric house. Carbon dating of two skeletons unearthed by archaeologists showed that the first, a man, had died in around 1600BC but had not been buried until a full six centuries later. The second skeleton, of a woman who had died in around 1300BC wasn't interred for another 300 years. It's thought they had initially been buried in a peat bog, peat being an excellent preservative. But why their contemporaries wanted to mummify them is a complete mystery. Were they great leaders, protectors or tribal warriors, on show for future generations to see? Another theory is that in ancient Scotland, people retained a kinship with the dead. Often ancestors, relatives and children were buried below the very houses in which people continued to live. (Keys, D; *Mummification in Bronze Age Britain*; www.bbc.co.uk/history; 2011)

Carrying on north, most of the houses were to my left on flat ground amongst the lochans. Looking west, the sky just goes on and on. With nothing to break the horizon, that entire coast of South Uist is one long sandy beach. To the east, a complete contrast: hills, a rocky coastline and deep penetrating sea lochs.

Passing the tiny settlements of Askernish and Mingarry, I came to the ruinous remains of the township of Milton and the cottage in which Flora MacDonald was born. The cottage walls have been repaired to a height of one metre with a large cairn built inside.

Flora MacDonald was, undoubtedly, Charles' most celebrated companion during his flight. Without her intervention he would most

Flora MacDonalds birthplace

certainly have been captured. Flora lived a full and eventful life. Interred in the tower of London after parting from Charles, she was released the following year. She married a highland chief and had ten children. Financial difficulties caused her to emigrate to North Carolina where her husband fought on the side of the British government during the American War of Independence. Flora eventually came back from the Americas and settled with her husband on Skye.

To keep the spirits up, I started belting out some Scotland football songs. I started with 'Ally's Tartan Army' from 1978 when we were going to win the World Cup. In 1982 when we weren't so sure, the song was 'I have a dream.' I finished with the 1998 anthem 'Wild Mountain Thyme' where the World Cup wasn't even mentioned.

My next stop was the Kildonan Museum where I searched in vain for Jacobite artefacts. The little museum had a good collection of domestic memorabilia and houses the Clanranald Stone, a sandstone tablet 80cm x 75cm carved with the Arms of Clanranald. Dating from the late 16th century, it had originally been built into one of the walls of a chapel in the township of Howmore. As the chapel fell into disrepair it was left lying against the remaining wall of the building and in 1990 was reported missing. Despite public appeals, nothing more was heard. Then in 1995 the parents of a young man who had died in his sleep contacted the British Museum. The stone was in his flat in London, which they had been clearing. Furthermore there were photographs of him and another unknown person removing it from the chapel. Happily, the stone is now back in the Uists and on permanent display.

I enjoyed coffee and shortbread in the museum café listening to country music, whilst writing some notes in my journal. Bliss.

For the first time since my arrival on the Western Isles the wind gradually died away. By lunchtime it was hot and quiet. The silence was stunning in this beautiful landscape, where the only movement was two golden eagles, circling high above.

I made my way to the ruins of Ormiclate castle in the vicinity of which Flora met the Prince for the first time. Despite being abandoned since 1715 on the death of the chief of Clanranald at the Battle of Sheriffmuir, the exterior walls of this two storey T-Plan mansion house were remarkably intact. With the ruins of farmhouses surrounding the castle the scene was reminiscent of a bombed out village from World War II.

O'Neil and MacEachen approached the shieling where Flora was staying and soon revealed the Prince to her. A plan was conceived by which she would take the Prince to Skye as her servant. Flora's stepfather was a captain of the government militia and could obtain a passport for Flora and 'Betty Burke', as the Prince was to be called, to travel between the islands.

From here the Prince retreated to the slopes of Hecla, six kilometres away where he hid while Flora went to Nunton to enlist the help of Lady Clanranald. Heading towards Hecla myself I deviated slightly to visit the township of Howbeg, where Neil MacEachen had been born.

By St Joseph's Church in Howbeg is an information board telling the story of Neil MacEachen and his son Alexander MacDonald. (Neil changed his surname during his exile in France). The remains of the black houses look over a lochan populated by geese, black-throated divers and oystercatchers.

I walked a short distance over the machair to the beach, where I camped among dunes. The wide expanse of sand stretched as far as the eye could see. I had the place to myself as I lay reading on the sand in the soft glow of a glorious sunset.

I retrieved fresh water from nearby Howmore Hostel, a lovely little thatched cottage run by the Gatliff Trust, a charitable organisation who operate three hostels in the Western Isles, with one also in Berneray and one on Harris, giving young people in particular the chance to experience remote crofting communities.

This little settlement had been an important centre of ecclesiastical activity. There are a whole series of remains of churches and chapels built throughout the last 800 years. These include Clanranald's chapel dating back to 1574, which originally housed the Clanranald stone. The present day church of 1866 sits on a knoll of high ground overlooking the site.

Back at my tent amongst the dunes I was concerned that the cattle roaming freely would trample me during the night. I'm a born worrier. The lull of the waves eventually swept my worries away and I dreamed happy dreams.

The next day I headed for Hecla (606m), which along with its neighbour Ben Mhor (Big mountain, 620m) dominate the waist of South Uist, and are far and away the largest hills on the island. The weather was bright again although the wind was back. Stormy weather was expected later in the afternoon so I wanted to get away quickly.

I returned to the main road, and followed a track east towards Ben Mhor. The path soon disappeared and I picked my way across boggy, marshy ground with pools of water reminding me of the dead marshes from the Lord of the Rings. There were no dead Viking warriors staring up at me, although without doubt, they could be in there, preserved in the peat.

I skirted round Maola Breac a foothill of Ben Mhor and headed along Glenn Dorchaidh. Near the head of the glen I climbed steadily through the heather onto the top of a shoulder of Benn Corradale, this smaller peak being sandwiched between Hecla and Beinn Mhor. Dropping my pack, I followed the wide undulating and rocky ridge to the steep upper flank of Hecla which I ascended zigzag fashion. The summit was crowned with rocks and there were spectacular views. Flat Benbecula was laid out before me and beyond that North Uist and Harris. To the west the beautiful sandy beaches stretched out for miles. To the east I could see over the Minch to the Isle of Skye. To the south, Beinn Mhor dominated. Had Charles wanted an idea of the positions of any forces that were out hunting him, then this was the place to be.

From the Slopes of Hecla, Charles had made his way north to Loch Sgiopoirt where he was rowed over to Wiay, before eventually meeting up with Flora on Benbecula. Before I followed I was going to visit Glen Corradale where Charles had spent three relatively happy weeks hidden and out of reach of Government forces prior to his trip to Loch Boisdale.

The wind was really getting up so I didn't linger on the summit and descended down to my rucksack and a sheltered lunch behind some large rocks. Forty minutes later the tormenting wind had intensified and I could hardly stand on the ridge without fear of being buffeted off the edge. I abandoned plans to climb Benn Corradale and instead dropped into Glen Usinish.

Descending quickly from the ridge, the wind soon abated and I found myself by the shores of a lochan that filled the glen floor. The slopes to my right were extremely steep, rocky and crag covered, but I had to find a way over this long spur of Ben Corradale to reach Charles' hidden glen. I continued east alongside the lochan heading towards the coast.

Eventually I found a section of hillside that I thought was worth a try. There was a stream, unmarked on my map, working its way down the slopes. I followed the edge of this stream upwards on steep muddy

Benn Corradale from Hecla

banks. Avoiding a waterfall, I continued along the slope to a steep dry gully. Scrambling upwards, with Meg the mountain goat ahead, I soon found myself on top of the spur and overlooking the sea. I worked my way southwards along this headland on steep but not exposed slopes to the holy grail of Glen Corradale.

A steep sided V-shaped glen, from the shore right to the head, this remote and sheltered valley was difficult to access, no matter from which direction you approached from.

Charles may have walked or sailed into Glen Corradale, but here he was able to holiday for a while from the stresses of being pursued. Instead he became hunter rather than hunted, stalking and shooting the abundant game that was available.

Clanranald visited him and provided a new set of highland clothes. MacDonald of Boisdale, a hardened drinker, also arrived but was unable to keep up with the Prince during a bout of imbibing and was comatose on the floor before morning.

Being in one place also allowed him to send out men to find out the state of the country. However the news was not good. Any armed resistance from the Highlanders had dissipated and the government troops were killing, raping and burning their way through the territories of his supporters.

The extent of the massive manhunt now on to catch him was also made plain. Thousands of troops were combing the Highlands and Islands for him and nine ships from the British Navy were patrolling the western seaboard to prevent his flight to France. However there was little Charles could do about this dangerous turn of events; he consoled himself with the fact that when he returned to France he would put things right.

I made my way to some ruins just above the stream. The houses had been butt 'n' ben type buildings. Later in my travels I spoke with a crofter whose relations had come from this glen, which must have been a tough and inhospitable place to survive. On the marshy floor there was virtually no flat ground and access down to the shore was steep and awkward with no natural harbour among the rocks. Only one or two of the ruins were on level ground, the others were perched on slopes above the stream. A small flattish area of ground had been walled in, probably for growing some crops.

Glen Corradale Cave

I was looking for a ruin in which there was a souterrain, a tunnel that ran underneath the house, accessed by moving a boulder to reveal the entrance. This tunnel would probably have been used for storage or possibly even hiding. My exploration was curtailed as the rain started to fall quite heavily and I sought out Charlie's cave for shelter. I found it in the face of some cliffs just above and to the north of the stream, but it was already occupied. A deer had taken shelter and died here. The carcass was still covered in flesh and matted fur. The cave was a D-shaped recess in the cliff and the smell within was overbearing.

Forewarned of a storm approaching, I set up my tent within one of the ruins, the walls of which were still one metre high and strong and secure. Although the cave is named after Charles, the contemporary accounts tell of him staying at a cottage.

The feelings of loneliness and isolation were strong here. An empty glen, howling wind, driving rain, hemmed in by steep hillsides, no sign of life. As well as the deer there were three sheep carcasses in the near vicinity in various states of decay. The ruins were a sad reminder that a community had once lived here. Children had played by the stream, shouting and shrieking as men and women went about their daily chores.

I wanted to talk to someone so I cranked up the satellite phone. However despite repeated attempts to connect I could only get through once and even then managed only one short burst of conversation with my daughter Kara. Enough to say I was OK and that was it.

But I wasn't OK. I was miserable. I wanted to experience some of the contentment that the Prince enjoyed when he was here. Of course he had escaped for the time being from government forces, so the pressure was off. He had companionship, he had supplies of food and alcohol, he could indulge in his favourite pastime, hunting. He had shelter; he had hope for the future. He was away from the reality of the reprisals that the government were inflicting upon his supporters.

I retired to my tent to await my fate.

The storm didn't disappoint. It was terrifying. The whole evening and throughout the night, the wind howled and the rain lashed down. Even with the pegs of my tent secured by boulders I was sure it would be blown away. It flapped noisily and shook continuously throughout the night. Unable to move without touching the billowing and wet sides of the canvas I lay in a trance, waiting, worrying, and hoping.

By 6am the storm had blown itself out. The tent, Meg and I had survived. After that night I never worried about my tent again. I had been in my sleeping bag for nearly twelve hours but I had hardly slept. I packed up quickly and retraced my footsteps out of Glen Corradale. I didn't stop for breakfast or to look about further, I wanted out of this forsaken valley.

Frank McGlynn in his excellent biography of the Prince said that Charles experienced massive psychological highs and lows whilst in Corradale, exacerbated by the plentiful supplies of brandy. Despite my lack of drink I felt similar emotions. From the bliss of an evening at the beach to the horror of the storm in the glen. All within 24 hours.

I headed north back to Glen Usinish over the steep ground above the shore. The ground was much wetter and the chances of slipping much greater following all the rain. I found the same gully as the previous day, now running with water, and I slithered down the channel.

Back in Glen Usinish, I followed the stream coming from the loch looking for a place to cross. The waters were swollen and tumbling forcefully downhill whilst any potential stepping-stones had been submerged so I bided my time. Where the stream met the sea it at last became shallow enough, widening out as it flowed over the rocky beach. I still had to ford it three times with my boots on in order to get the rucksack and the dog over. Usinish bothy was nearby and I headed there.

Overlooking the shingle beach of Usinish Bay I found a two-room cottage with a corrugated iron roof. What a blessing to escape the outside conditions for a while. The first room was a storeroom and the second was a well-stocked howf with bunk beds and a little stove. There were packets and tins of food, matches, candles and even a bottle of diluting juice. Although it was just past nine o'clock I was already soaked from the rain, the sweat and the river. I stripped off to dry out, and hung my clothes to drip dry. The room was Baltic and I plundered a tin of sardines as I sat naked huddled round my stove waiting for my water to boil.

Duly heated up by porridge and coffee, I took stock of my situation. It had been a rough night and I had suffered from some grim forebodings. Despite my fears I had survived, escaped the glen and I was now cheery, comfortable and out of the wind and rain. There was no climbing today so once I stepped outside again, the conditions could throw whatever they wanted at me.

From the slopes of Hecla, Charles headed to Loch Skiport guided by Neil MacEachen where he was rowed over to Wiay and then on to Benbecula.

Following the Prince to Loch Skiport I would go back onto tarmac roads to cross the causeway into Benbecula. I was heading back towards civilisation and possibly even a shop of some kind. The thought of the luxuries that a shop could provide was like a kick up the backside and I got myself together and headed outside duly refreshed and motivated.

With hills to my left running down to the sea, and numerous streams running off them I expected the ground to be boggy and marshy. It was. I made my way north past a jutting headland onto which was squeezed a row of three hills. On the edge of this headland, the most easterly part of South Uist, is a Stevenson lighthouse sitting atop sheer cliffs, looking like it is going to slip into the sea at any moment.

I was grateful for a track made by some brave soul in an all-terrain vehicle. Not marked on my map, it made its way from the bothy up and over the hillsides, under rock embankments, over rock escarpments, through marshy and boggy ground, diving down to cross channels eroded by streams, before climbing back up on onto ridges with steep sides. A real roller coaster of a journey. Though it was faint in places, I managed to follow it all morning, reducing by half the time I had allowed to cross this difficult territory.

Still on the path and under the northern cliffs of Maol Martaig, I gazed over to my right to Acarsaid Falaich, the hidden harbour, where at one point the Prince's boat sought shelter. This remote inlet is still used today by modern yachts seeking a harbour or shelter from inclement weather.

Descending now, north of Loch Bein the ground became a quagmire. Trying to jump from grassy tussock to grassy tussock was tiring and the rucksack jarred on my back with every bounce. Eventually I was past caring and with my gators having slipped round my ankles I ploutered on regardless, through the waterlogged ground.

By early afternoon the sun was out, the wind had dropped and I was on a footpath following the shore of Loch Skiport. Wild Hebridean ponies living freely down by the shore ignored my presence.

I met a couple of people out for a day's walking, who had spent

Hebridean ponies

the night in a caravan further south at Loch Aineort. I hadn't spoken to anyone for two days so I was eager to talk. They said they were sure their caravan was going to blow away and were quite incredulous that I had survived unscathed in my tent.

The track led on to a B-class road and I had lunch by Loch Druidibeg Nature Reserve. Lying back for a few moments I mulled over my progress for the day so far, pleased that I had covered 13kms. My difficulties were over as I could now follow the main road north to Lionaclet where I could get provisions at the shop. I craved fresh food: bread, cheese and milk. Plain porridge made with water was becoming abhorrent at breakfast times; I needed sugar or salt to liven it up. The thought of these luxuries and a hot shower at the campsite drove me on the next 13km.

Worried that the shop might close at 6pm I rushed along the A865, past 'Our Lady of the Isles.' This magnificent eight-metre statue by Hew Lorimer represents the Virgin Mary and overlooks the Ministry of Defence rocket range.

In the 1950s Canon John Morrison, 'Father Rocket', led the opposition to the proposed MOD site which was to be large scale and would see local people removed from their homes. The protestors also thought it would damage the faith, language and culture of the island community. The scale of the plans was subsequently cut back and the military operations have proved good for the area, bringing in well-paid jobs. Some people, having completed their posting here, remained on the island, helping to strengthen the population.

With the Western Isles being so flat you can see bad weather approaching (and leaving!) and I prepared for a rainstorm as I saw the clouds rolling in. Eventually the deluge defeated me and I took shelter at a covered bus stop. But it soon passed, and the sun came out once more.

I crossed the causeway into Benbecula in time to make the shop at Creagorry where I purchased fresh food and some treats for Meg. She had been a star over the past few days. Never complaining, she covered the ground easily and patiently listened to all my troubles.

The evening was sunny and dry, and although my feet and legs hurt from a long days walking, I was happy. My stomach was crammed full, and my tent, sleeping bag and waterproofs had all been dried on a washing line at the campsite.

The following morning I felt quite the opposite and couldn't muster up any enthusiasm. I dawdled along minor and unclassified roads towards Creagastrom where I picked up the Prince's trail.

On 24 June Charles had landed on Benbecula once more having been rowed over from the Isle of Wiay. It was in this vicinity that the Prince was probably put ashore, most likely at one of the tidal islands just to the east, from where he walked onto Benbecula proper.

Reaching Creagastrom, now a private jetty for the Scottish Salmon Company, I looked over to Wiay and imagined the Prince being rowed over in the half dark of an early morning. Tired and exhausted after rough living and continual movement for the past three weeks, he had one more journey to make before leaving the Western Isles for good.

I turned around and headed over rough ground towards Loch Uskavagh, hopefully taking a similar route to the one the Prince followed. I aimed for the small rise of Drum na Lice. The ground underfoot varied between knee high heather and peaty marshland. I was becoming an expert bogtrotter by now, able to tell the firm ground from the soft so I hopped and jumped my way between a myriad of small lochans as I headed northwest. At the little knoll I surveyed the scene. I was in the centre of one large area of marshland with nothing but a complex series of interconnected lochans surrounding me. Benbecula's only hill, Rueval provided me with a point to fix on. Heading north I passed the ruined cottage of Lidistrom on the southern shore of Loch Uskavagh. A number of such cottages remain around the loch on the eastern seaboard, and were occupied until the 1960s. Families had made a living from sheep and shellfish and a little land cultivation, but the lack of a road to this part of Benbecula meant that as pressure for land eased off due to falling population, people were able to find less remote parts to croft.

Charles had a nightmare journey at night here, losing a shoe in his travels. I had sunny weather but could appreciate the difficulties in wet or dark conditions when it was impossible to tell the firm from the boggy ground. Arriving at Loch Uskavagh he remained in the area for two days avoiding local militia and awaiting Flora MacDonald. On one occasion with the enemy nearby he hid by a rock that gave him virtually no cover from the rain, nor the ravenous midges. He was heard to utter hideous cries and complaints as he waited for the soldiers to move on.

Towards Rueval

Eventually Flora MacDonald and Lady Clanranald arrived. They shared supper and brought servants clothes to disguise him as an Irish maid. He was to be called Betty Burke. Large numbers of soldiers were now in Benbecula looking for the Prince and when it was reported that the notoriously cruel Captain Scott and a large company of men had landed nearby, the meal was abandoned and the party fled to the north shore of the loch, the Rosinish peninsula.

The tide was in as I approached Loch Uskavagh, so I couldn't ford a narrow tidal channel and I made my way to its western end where at a little stream flowing into the loch I picked some fresh mussels. Continuing by the loch the ground remained difficult until I reached a blessed track. This footpath connected the Rosinish peninsula through the lochans and around Rueval with the rest of Benbecula to the west. It was originally an old kelp road where kelp would be collected and transported. On the path lay the remains of a lamb that had been ripped apart. As there are no foxes (or hooded crows) on Benbecula it may well have been eagle fodder.

Later, I climbed Rueval, surrounded by almost 100 lochans. It was on the slopes of this hill that Charles hid while waiting for Flora to arrive from Nunton House.

Camping by one of the lochans, I boiled my mussels for five minutes. They were simply amazing. To get my food from the land was pure Ray Mears. I reflected that I was two weeks into my walk. My health was good and my feet were holding out. I was trying to savour every moment, and although I missed loved ones, I knew in my heart of hearts that this was an opportunity that might never come round again.

For my final day on the Western Isles I was in the company of Alasdair MacEachen who was going to guide me to the spot where Charles left for Skye.

Walking on the footpath he pointed out Prince Charles' Well, a stream running off the southern slope of Rueval which I had read about and seen a picture of, in Drummond Norrie's book of 1902, but not heard of since.

Passing by concrete foundations at Minish, the remoteness made it hard to believe that these were remains of a school, which had served the community working the crofts that were created by the splitting of Nunton Farm after World War 1. The upper part of the building was made from iron sheets and when the school closed they were transported to North Uist and reused.

The footpath continued on into Rosinish peninsula, the place where Charles first landed on the Western Isles after sailing over from the mainland. He landed here again after his unsuccessful trip to Stornoway. It was here also that he left the Western Isles for the final time, on 28 June 1746. The fact that Charles visited the peninsula so often showed that during the period of his flight this was a remote area. It may well have been that the Clanranalds, who owned the land, used it as a hunting forest.

Soon we reached the remains of a house by the shore where Duncan MacRae, the last resident, had lived until the 1960s. With the slate roof virtually intact the two-storey house with storm windows was in good condition, considering it has been unoccupied for 50 years.

Alasdair guided me to the eastern part of the peninsula known as Cuidhe Thearlich or Charlie's Fold, a little rocky inlet at 878530 on the Ordnance Survey Landranger Map. This was the actual leaving place and from here the Prince sailed over the sea to Skye. Other than Flora whose maid he was disguised as, Charles' only companion was MacEachen. Sailors made up the rest of the crew.

Charlie's Fold

Returning west to Aird, I visited the croft that had been in Alistair's family for 266 years passing down from father to son. Alasdair's descendant fought for the Jacobites at Culloden and after returning home his chief Clanranald gave him a croft holding on the western part of Benbecula in appreciation of his services. Now as then, sheep are reared and I watched one of the next generation being born. Within 15 minutes it was licked clean and on its feet.

Finally I visited Nunton House, home of the Clanranald Chiefs in 1746. The 18th century L-plan building was erected to replace Ormiclate Castle on South Uist. It has been recently restored and is now a high quality bunkhouse. I visited the kitchen that retained the original fireplace. It was from this room that Lady Clanranald lifted the servant clothes to provide Charles with the disguise for which he is so well known.

Following the Prince to Skye, I took a bus for Lochmaddy from where I would get a ferry to return to Uig. It seemed a lifetime since I had left Skye; it had been nine glorious days.

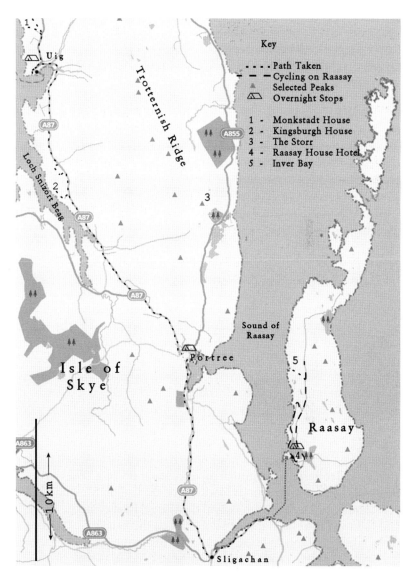

Northern Skye and Raasay

CHAPTER 4

The Isles of Skye and Raasay

ON A BEAUTIFUL Spring afternoon I travelled over the sea to Skye on the giant 5,500 tonne MV *Hebrides*. Although my boat was slightly bigger, this was the journey that the song fondly recalls. The two-hour sailing would take me from Loch Maddy to Uig, near to where the Prince landed on 29 June 1746, ten weeks after the battle of Culloden.

The Prince left the Western Isles disguised as Flora's maid and MacEachen travelled as Flora's guide. Charles regaled Flora, MacEachen and the six-man crew with songs such as 'The King Shall Have his Ane Again' and 'The Twenty-Ninth of May.' Overnight the sailors rowed, and then as the wind picked up, they sailed across the Little Minch to the north-west tip of Skye on the Waternish peninsula. At this point they were spotted by a group of government soldiers on the shore, but due to the low tide, and rough sea conditions they could not launch their own boat to follow. The Prince's boat put in further round Waternish point to allow the sailors some rest. Finally they rowed across Loch Snizort to a point of land close to Monkstadt House on the Trotternish Peninsula, where they arrived mid-afternoon.

My own uneventful journey ended when the ferry docked at Uig, and I headed back to Uig Bay Campsite where I took up lodgings once more. It was early evening and I decided to make a start on Charles' journey by heading up to Princes Point, where the boat had put ashore. The landing place was just a few kilometres north of Uig, and further along the Trotternish Peninsula. Skye is made up of a series of such peninsulas emanating from its black heart, the Cuillin Mountains.

Climbing up a steep path behind the village, I joined the main road, and followed it for a couple of kilometres to the hamlet of Totscore. I met a farmer and sought his advice about crossing the fields to the shore.

Eying Meg, the farmer warned me to be careful, as the cattle were likely to attack the dog.

'If the cows see you and charge, let go the dog's lead', he advised me, 'she'll find her way to safety.'

'Is there a bull?' I asked hesitantly.

'Yep, there's bull too.'

Final question, 'How did you get your injury?'

'One of the cows kicked me a few days ago.' The farmer was limping heavily and in obvious discomfort.

Never, in the field of Jacobite exploration, have a man and his rather puzzled dog sprinted across a field as quickly as Meg and I did that evening. The cows at the other side of the field looked over quite unconcerned as we sped past. The 400m dash started as a sprint and ended as a stagger and I reached the sea with only the rocky shoreline preventing me from collapsing in a breathless heap.

Landing here, the Prince had hoped to receive help from Lady MacDonald of Sleat. Her husband's house, Monkstadt, was just a few hundred metres to the north-east. MacDonald of Sleat was the man whose support Charles had counted on upon his arrival in Scotland the previous year, but who had declined to join the Rising. At this juncture, MacDonald was in Fort Augustus meeting with the Duke of Cumberland. His wife however, was more steadfast in her support and had provided help and information to Charles whilst he was hiding in the Western Isles.

The Prince's Point

Charles waited by the shore still dressed in maid's clothes. Flora and MacEachen went to visit the house, to find that Lady Margaret had guests, and among them was a captain of the local militia, whose role was to watch the coastline for any boats carrying suspected Jacobites. Luckily for the Prince, the captain was rather lax that Sunday afternoon. Lady Margaret was horrified that Charles was only a stone's throw away and in imminent danger of capture. It was quickly decided that the Prince should be taken to the Isle of Raasay, where he could find shelter with his supporters, the MacLeods. Sailing round to Raasay was considered too dangerous due to the number of lookouts posted round the coastline, so crossing Skye on foot was agreed. The journey began with the Prince being spirited away by Lady Margaret's factor, MacDonald of Kingsburgh, who escorted Charles to his house, 12kms away. MacEachen and Flora caught up with the Prince on the road south. Still disguised as Betty Burke, Charles was berated by his companions for the unladylike way in which he carried himself, which in turn, would draw the attention of any passers-by.

Having regained my puff, I crossed a couple of cattle-free fields to reach Monkstadt House, home of the MacDonald Chiefs from the 1730s to 1815. I had seen some pictures of its ruinous condition in guidebooks so I was amazed to see a beautifully restored two-storey L-plan country house.

Monkstadt House

I knocked on the door but there was no reply, so I took a wander past some nearby cottages and some partially restored steadings. All very interesting. Whilst nosing about, I captured the attention of one of the occupants who came out to see what I was up to. It turned out to be the owner of Monkstadt house, Ian McQueen, who had restored it from the pitiful ruin it had become since the roof was removed in the 1950s. Restoration had been time consuming and costly, a real labour of love, and Ian deserves great credit for saving an important part of Skye's heritage. Now completed, the house was on sale for £675,000. We chatted for some time about the MacDonalds, Jacobites and the economic recession. Ian related a story to me about some of the atrocities committed by government troops in the aftermath of the Rising. Not only, as one officer said, did the soldiers 'hang or shoot anyone suspected of hiding the prince,' but they attacked women and children too.

Not so very far away at Iona, in 697AD, a Columban Monk, Adoman introduced a 'Law of Innocents' that protected women, children and other innocents from the ravages of war. This was agreed upon by contemporary Pictish and Scottish Kings. In 1746 the British Government was operating a hideous policy of retribution that had been outlawed in the so-called Dark Ages, 1,000 years earlier.

The Dark Ages had returned, quite literally, to Skye when I said goodbye and left the steadings. In total darkness, I tiptoed back to Uig across the silent fields. I was half expecting to be accosted by a bull or possibly even an American werewolf. As the farmer had mentioned earlier, Meg would be fine. She could outrun me any day. I was smiling in the dark, thinking of Billy Connolly telling one of his classics; about the guy being chased by a lion who stopped to change into his training shoes, whilst his breathless friend says 'You'll never outrun a lion.'

His pal replied, 'I don't care, as long as I can outrun you.'

The next morning, having restocked with some provisions that I had left at the campsite, I headed south along the main road, towards Kingsburgh House. I was encouraged by the change of scenery, rolling green fields surrounding the crofting township of Earlish. A distinct change from the yellows and browns of the heather to which I had become accustomed to, on the east coast of Benbecula and South Uist.

Marked on the map 7km south of Uig was Prince Charles Well. Leaving the road at the bridge over the River Hinnisdal, I followed a

Duncan's Emporium on the road to Kingsburgh

farm track west until I came to the waters of Lon Ruadh. The stream went through a thick stand of birch trees where my rucksack caught on every low branch. At the location of the well, the stream widened to a fording point, where the Prince may have stopped for a drink. Other than that there was nothing but gorse bushes and cow dung.

Further down, and just off the main road was the clachan of Kingsburgh and past a scattering of crofts was Kingsburgh House. I approached down a long, tree-lined drive with many fallen victims of recent storms on either side. At the side of the house the owner, Emilia Colbourne, who had been busy gardening, met me. She explained that her mother and stepfather purchased the house in 1951, and she had lived there ever since. After some negotiations she led me round to the front of the house and on seeing it I understood her reluctance. Kingsburgh is a three bay house with two storeys and an attic level. The protruding centre bay has a crow-stepped top. Unfortunately most of the house has fallen into disrepair and is in a sad and dilapidated condition. Emilia lives in a recently restored, single storey part of the east wing. Despite pressure from local property developers Miss Colbourne refuses to sell up and she made me very welcome whilst explaining her family's history. Despite the houses links with Bonnie Prince Charlie, Emilia had little time for the young Stuart and had agreed with the historian who said the Rising 'was the maddest scheme in the whole of Scottish history.'

Whilst at Kingsburgh, Charles spent a happy evening eating, drinking brandy, and smoking with his host. He then slept in a bed for the first time in many weeks. Most accounts place the house in which Charles stayed at a site nearer the loch shore, although Emilia showed me some photographs of renovation work that took place on her current quarters, which uncovered an archway believed to date from the 15th century. During his lifetime, Emilia's stepfather had become convinced that the current house was the one in which Charles stayed.

Flora MacDonald went on to live at Kingsburgh House, when she married Kingsburgh's son, and it was there that they raised their ten children. During their tour of 1776, James Boswell and Dr Samuel Johnson met Flora here. Dr Johnson was impressed by Flora and said of her, '...a name that will be mentioned in history, and if courage and fidelity be virtues, mentioned with honour.'

The halfway point of my day's walk was at the small crofting community of Romesdal, where I had a late lunch of Hebridean lamb chops. I had been given them as a gift whilst on Benbecula and had cooked them at the B&B that morning. They were a delightful change from my usual dried food lunch, which was usually either couscous or risotto. Thereafter picking bits of meat from my teeth kept me occupied whilst I continued my journey.

On my left were hillsides leading up to the Trotternish ridge, a high spine of land with cliff faces on its east side. The ridge is the longest geological landslip in Britain with a length of 32km. It encompasses the atmospheric landscape of the Quiraing, incredible rock formations including the Needle and the Prison. Also making up part of the Trotternish ridge is Storr Hill, which overlooks The Old Man of Storr, a 50m rock pinnacle and one of Skye's best-known landmarks.

The final kilometres along the increasingly busy main road were a bit of a slog. The tendon on my right big toe was painful, having hurt it the previous day. In addition, my shoulders were sore from the weight and balance of the rucksack. No matter how I seemed to adjust it, my left shoulder always seemed to bear the majority of the weight.

When the rucksack developed an annoying squeak, I really started to lose the plot.

On large sections of the A87 there was very little verge on which to walk, certainly not enough for Meg and I to walk side by side. I was forced onto the road, stepping off it to accommodate oncoming cars. Being in pain and frustrated by the rhythmic squeak I took it out on the drivers and waited until the last minute to move. In return I received non-complementary gesticulations for my efforts, each one giving me a bit of grim satisfaction.

As Portree got closer my mood improved. Lots of good memories came flooding back, having spent many happy family holidays here. The town is the largest settlement on Skye with a population of around 2,500 out of the 10,000 on the island as a whole. It has a good variety of accommodation including a campsite, hostel, B&Bs, budget and quality hotels. The highlight of the town is the picturesque natural harbour surrounded by brightly coloured guesthouses and shops.

On my first holiday in Skye, my wife and I had a night out in Portree sampling the various bars in the town. The following morning I was too rough to make breakfast although Nicola managed it. I awoke with a shock to find a total stranger tickling my feet at the end of the bed. It was the bloody maid, who had found a novel way to get hung-over guests out of their beds and out of her road.

On another occasion, Nicola and I were sitting in the doctor's surgery with our daughter, Sophie, who was one year old at the time and had broken out in a rash. An elderly lady with a bit of facial fuzz and a red jacket was sitting in the waiting room with us. To our horror, Sophie started pointing at the lady, calling her 'Santa.' Soon we were biting our fingers trying not to laugh, praying that we would be called to the doctor's room. When eventually it was our turn, the doctor examining Sophie pulled out a book to determine her condition. Whilst he was reading from the book my wife and I looked at each other, both of us thinking 'No Way Man.'

It's the outdoors activities that have brought me back to Skye, time and time again. Climbing in the Cuillin, visiting the historic sites and exploring the natural wonders like the Quiraing.

Charles arrived at McNab's Inn on 30 June, having changed out of his female garb just before entering the village. Flora and MacEachen had done more than possibly could have been expected of them, and now took their leave. The Prince said to Flora that hopefully they would yet meet in the palace of St James in London. She was later arrested and imprisoned in the Tower of London for her part in the Prince's escape. She was well enough looked after, unlike many other captives who were abysmally treated.

After the Rising there were 3,470 Jacobite prisoners in gaols and prison. Of these, 120 were executed, although this included 38 deserters from the government army. Shockingly, 772 died in prison from 'wounds, fever, starvation and neglect.' Almost 1,000 were transported to the colonies in indentured employment, where the prisoners worked without wages for a set number of years. This would typically be on a plantation. Two hundred and twenty two prisoners were banished from the country. Fifty-eight escaped and most of the rest were eventually released.

Flora MacDonald was released in 1747 to find herself a heroine for the part she played in the Prince's escape. MacEachen remained free and sailed to France 11 weeks later, never to return to Scotland.

McNab's Inn is now called the Royal Hotel, where the staff

The Royal Hotel

warmly welcomed us, with Meg in particular getting lots of attention. My large warm room overlooked the harbour and I pranced around naked in the abundant space. This was just immense after the struggles of getting changed in a tiny tent and squeezing into a tiny sleeping bag feeling like a legless caterpillar. After a hot bath, the strains and pains of earlier were soon forgotten.

In the morning I was first in the restaurant and the friendly waiter buzzed around chatting away and giving me some company as I ate. Finding out I had a canine companion he organised breakfast for Meg. She probably thought she had died and gone to heaven when I got back to the room and put the chopped up bacon, sausage, haggis and black pudding in front of her. As usual she wolfed it down in one go, much to my annoyance. What a waste!

I headed down to the harbour, to see what was happening. Although there was a choice of leisure cruises available, nothing was going to Raasay until the following day. Plan B was to get back on the main road, and head south to Sconser where I could catch the regular ferry service.

The Prince had better luck than me and sailed from Portree over to Glam on Raasay accompanied by Captain Malcolm MacLeod, whose account of his time with the Prince was published in the Lyon in Mourning. Also present were two of the Laird of Raasay's sons, one of whom had been shot in the shoulder at Culloden.

From this harbour the emigration boats left which made a significant contribution to reducing the island's population from a high in 1841 of over 23,000.

After purchasing some supplies at a supermarket and then at a well-stocked outdoor shop, I headed out of Portree, passing the Aros centre, which serves local people and tourists alike with films, concerts and exhibitions. I would have stopped for a visit but I was on a mission to catch the 3pm ferry. On my left, Ben Tianavaig (413m) stood out on its own dominating the south side of Portree Bay. Ahead the road entered Glen Varragil. As it was a Saturday morning the road out of Portree was relatively quiet in comparison to yesterday's teatime approach. Feeling fresh, my body seemed to find a natural rhythm that ate up the distance.

Soon I had my first decent sighting of the Black Cuillin, Skye's beautiful and challenging mountain range. The jagged bare rock peaks

Meg and I ready to set off in the company of a few Jacobites from the Culloden Battlefield Centre.

Culloden (1746) by David Morier. Jacobite prisoners were reputedly used as models. Note they wear different colour tartans.

Looking towards the head of Loch Arkaig with Glen Pean going into the distance.

Glen Pean, one of the roughest glens in Scotland. A flooded valley floor, two lochans and a large rockfall block progress.

Gleann an Obain Bhig. The setting is dramatic, the terrain is unruly and the location remote and timeless.

Ormiclate Castle in the background. Burned to a shell on the same day the chief, Clanranald, was killed at the Battle of Sherrifmuir (1715).

The Prince spent three weeks in inaccessible Glen Corradale.
Note the cave in the middle of the cliff face.

Elgol, with the Cuillin ridge in the backgorund. Charles arrived in Elgol
after a mighty overnight march from Portree.

Eilean na Glasschoile. Charles waited on this tiny island whilst his companions went ashore to find out if it was safe to land on the Knoydart peninsula.

The Silver Sands of Morar. A beautiful location, with a large cave nearby.

Looking over Loch Hourn on another beautiful day. In the distance Ladhar Bheinn at over 1,000 metres.

Glen Affric, the glen of countless colours. It was truly stunning on the day I passed through.

Approaching Loch Arkaig once again. On the other side of the loch is Glen Mallie.

Glen Tarsuinn goes off in the distance. Often when the tent went up
the dog went down.

Snow on Ben Alder in Badenoch. Culra Bothy in the foreground.

Inside Corryhully bothy. A fabulous night for Meg and I in front of a roaring fire.

A happy reunion with my family. The cairn marks the place where Charles
left Scotland for the final time.

were dusted in snow giving them definition and an ominous look. The C-shaped ridge is only seven miles long but features 11 Munros. None of them are completely straightforward and even the easiest peak requires some scrambling. The most awkward summit is the Inaccessible Pinnacle of Sgurr Dearg (Red peak). Many have called it the hardest of all Scotland's Munros and it is one that the original Munroist, Sir Hugh Munro, never climbed. It was another 134 years after Charles passed by that brothers Lawrence and Charles Pilkington, of glass making fame, conquered it.

By mid-afternoon I had followed the main road to the Sligachan Hotel at the foot of the Cuillin, a refuge for climbers and tourists since 1830. One New Year's holiday, Nicola, my brother in law, his wife and myself had a night out at the hotel. The most memorable part of the evening was the wild journey on the late bus back to Portree. Having had a great time at the disco, or listening to live music, people continued the party on the way home. Back at Portree, my brother-in-law and I procured shopping trolleys for racing round the square. Girls inside, boys pushing. The police intervened, banning us instantly before we could damage the messages.

In the Prince's day, a building slightly nearer Loch Sligachan was

Sligachan ahead

in existence. Fearful of capture, he gave it a body swerve. Fearful of missing my ferry, I did the same.

Toiling, and thoroughly sick of walking on a main road, I made it at last to Sconser where I made my connection for the short trip across the sound of Raasay. Looking over to the island, the houses were nestled between the shoreline and the forested hillsides. Dun Caan, an unmistakable flat topped mountain was in the distance, poking out like a chimney.

Landing at the new pier in Churchton Bay, I found my way up to the Raasay House Hotel where Meg and I dumped our bags. I hired a mountain bike to take me up to Glam, where Prince Charles spent the night after sailing over from Portree.

I watched Meg carefully, initially concerned that I was pushing her a bit too hard considering we had already walked 18km. My fears were unwarranted, she kept up fine as I cycled gently north. Raasay was beautiful and green, the sun was out and I felt totally re-invigorated as I travelled along the quiet coastal road with great views back across the sound to Ben Lee, and the striking escarpment on the eastern side of Ben Tianavaig.

Twenty-three kilometres long and five kilometres across its widest point, Raasay has a population of around 200. Her most famous son is Sorley Maclean (1911–1996) the Gaelic poet.

Raasay is also the location of Calum's Road, a 2.8km section of road built in extremely difficult terrain by a very determined man because the local council wouldn't do it. An amazing feat of engineering by any man, never mind someone in his 60s with just a 'How to...' book and the most basic of tools. The subject has inspired songs, a book and a play by the National Theatre of Scotland.

After Culloden, a regiment of government militia raised by MacLeod of Dunvegan gave this island and the innocent populace a hammering as part of the reprisals for the local chief having supported the Rising. Of the 300 cottages on the island not one remained with a roof after the militia had visited their depredations. It has to be emphasised that these were MacLeods punishing MacLeods. Over 1,000 animals were driven off and slaughtered. The militia pillaged from one end of the island to another and starvation would kill even more. (Prebble, J; *Culloden*; Pimlico; London, 2002; page 222)

At Holoman Island, a small tidal island 100m off the shore, the road turned inland, taking a zigzag path uphill. Reaching a TV mast, the road then took a dip down to the old settlement of Brae and then a final climb uphill had me blowing hard to reach Glam. I had gained 200m in height giving great views over towards Portree Bay. There was only a farm in the vicinity, so like Charles, I did not linger.

At Glam the Prince spent just one evening in a small turf hut, realising that the island was too small to shelter him safely. He also saw first-hand – and could scarcely believe – the treatment that had been delivered upon the common people of the Highlands and Islands. Whilst hidden, he showed his own humanity by staying the hand of Malcolm MacLeod who was going to shoot a passing peddler, suspected of being a spy. 'God forbid that any poor man should suffer for us, if we can keep ourselves safe.' Fortunately the man passed by without looking into the hut.

Keeping the brakes on to allow Meg to keep up, I headed back downhill to Brae where I left the bike beside a couple of ruined cottages and a couple of deciduous trees. With eagles circling high above, I walked down the marked path towards Inver Bay entering a narrow gorge with steep sides, filled with birch and hazel trees. Following a burn I descended towards the river, the wooded slopes giving way to heather. As the ground levelled out I passed an ancient ruined cottage before reaching the beautiful Inver Bay. This small, sheltered and sandy bay, opposite Portree Bay seemed an ideal place for Charles to have landed before making his way up to Glam.

Charles, Prince of Wales, the current heir apparent, also landed on Raasay here. Prior to 1997, the Royal Family took an annual Hebridean cruise on board their yacht, *Britannia*. The bay at Inver was one of the deserted and remote beaches that the royal family enjoyed, and where complete privacy could be assured.

Stopping just for a couple of photos, I turned around and headed back uphill to the bike. I took an alternative route back to the Outdoor Centre via the Alan Evans Memorial Youth Hostel before descending down to Orchard Wood and then Borrodale wood. Arriving back at the outdoor centre I entered the bar at the same time as a lady with two dogs of her own. Meg loves human attention and will snuggle up to anyone who even looks her way. As usual, she broke the ice when

Inver Bay

people were around and I ended up chatting to Lyn, the owner of the dogs, who also happened to own the outdoor centre. She was very interested in my walk, asking lots of questions about my thoughts on the Rising.

Lyn had provided the boat that Bonnie Prince Charlie had used to sail to Glenfinnan in the 1995 re-enactment. The celebration had marked 250 years since the standard was raised. When asked by a hotel patron what role Raasay played in the Rising, Lyn explained to him about the MacLeod support and the horrors inflicted upon Raasay after Culloden. When discussing the Jacobite Rising in places directly affected by the aftermath, it is easy to feel outrage and to lay the blame for the empty glens at Cumberland's door. The violent wrenching apart of the clan system started the moment after Culloden, but it was the Highland Chiefs who prolonged the agony for a further 100 years in their quest to turn clan lands into profitable estates. After demonstrating the Jacobite handshake, Lyn offered me use of the outdoor centre's campsite complete with showering facilities, which I gladly accepted. Outdoor activities were being organised from the only hotel on the island, since in 2010, the purpose built outdoor centre burned to the ground, just as a four million pound refurbishment was nearing completion.

Walking to the campsite I pitched my tent and then realised that I had left Meg's bowl back at the hotel's public bar. Well, almost Meg's bowl! I had in fact, left Meg's bowl back on the Western Isles and she was now using *my* bowl to eat and drink from. We weren't sharing; I was eating directly from my cooking pot, which reduced heat loss anyway.

A tawny owl called from the trees as I headed through the gloom to the pub. The bright lights, visible from a distance formed a beacon, drawing me towards a warm, welcoming environment. It was now Saturday evening and when I opened the door there was chatter, laughter and happiness, a crowd of people all having a great time. I moseyed on in, picked up the bowl and spoke with some of the outdoor instructors for a few moments. One of them was convinced that Charlie had performed a highland dance on top of Dun Caan during his visit. This rather comical belief was not as far away from the truth as it first seemed. It transpired that it was Boswell and Dr Johnson who had climbed Dun Caan and on the flat summit, Boswell had danced a highland jig. A pint or two in the convivial atmosphere would have been an ideal way to end the day. However I had determined not to drink alcohol on my travels so I dragged myself away, regretting my pledge. The Prince had left the Highlands having developed a dependency on alcohol, and I knew within myself that a pint or two was never enough.

Back at the campsite, perched on a log, I savoured a cup of coffee, the lure of alcohol having abated. Content, I relaxed and looked out over the sound of Raasay to the lights of the township of Camustianavaig on the opposite shore. The temperature was mild, there were no midges, and today's unread newspaper lay in the tent awaiting. After a very productive day I was perfectly at peace with the surroundings and myself.

The following morning I had a long lie until 8am, still giving me plenty of time to catch the 10am ferry back to Skye. The walk back was a little longer than expected so I ended up jogging down to the pier. When I went to put a lead on Meg to get on the boat, there was no doggy rucksack. Looking around I couldn't see it and immediately started to panic. Shouting at Meg, she just cocked an ear when I demanded an explanation. It was almost 10 o'clock and the next ferry wasn't for another six hours. I put down my own rucksack, and ran around the area surrounding the pier, looking for it. It wasn't about, so I retraced my steps, sprinting back along the road. About 400m later there it was, lying by the roadside, with not a care in the world. Fortunately, Lyn was driving down to the pier at this moment and gave me a lift back to the ferry. Parting with a Jacobite handshake and a Jacobite rose for the journey, I boarded the ferry, sweaty but relieved.

The ticket inspector on the ferry was welcoming and took time to speak to a breathless hiker. Despite the day job requiring him to be on the water, in his spare time he was a keen kayaker. I told him about my walk and we started talking about Charlie. He didn't believe in the divine right of kings, which the Stuarts would have required had they been successful in getting back their throne. He also believed in a more modern form of religion than the authoritarian Episcopalianism that the Stuarts backed. I think he would have been fighting against me at Culloden.

Getting off the ferry I noticed Meg was limping. Pangs of guilt flooded through me for making her run the 16km yesterday while I cycled. I checked her out, more thoroughly than the last time, but there was nothing to see. As much to ease my guilt, as it was to ease her pain, I carried her rucksack for the rest of the day.

From Raasay, Charles sailed back towards Portree, amidst a storm that had the sailors urging the Prince to return whence they had come. Charles would not hear of it and sang a 'merry highland song' to help fortify the crew. Back on Skye he slept in a cowshed, and then walked towards Sligachan taking the route I had travelled the previous day. From there he continued on to Elgol on the south tip of the Strathaird peninsula where he hoped to get shelter from his supporters the McKinnons. It was a mighty overnight walk with Charles being guided by Malcolm MacLeod, and posing as his servant Lewie Caw. The Prince gave MacLeod his fine waistcoat, which would seem to have been the only item of his attire that was too fine for a servant to wear. As a servant should, Charles walked a suitable distance behind MacLeod and carried the little amount of baggage that they possessed. Noticing his discomfort Malcolm examined the Prince and removed 80 lice from his clothing; MacLeod says of the Prince 'that the fatigues

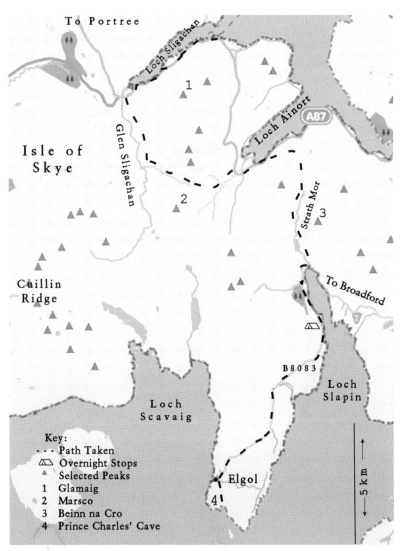

Sligachan to Elgol

and distresses he underwent signified nothing at all, because he was a single person; but when he reflected upon the many brave fellows who suffered in his cause, that, he behoved to own, did strike him to the heart, and did sink very deep with him.'

By returning to Sligachan I could catch up with the Prince again and although I had varied the order ever so slightly, I had still managed to cover the same ground. Soon I arrived at the head of Loch Sligachan and I entered the glen of the same name along a good stony path, with the Cuillin ridge on my right and the cone shaped hill, Glamaig on my left. I made my way southwards until Marsco (Seagull hill) and Sgurr nan Gillean (Peak of the young men) were towering above me, giant sentinels guarding the gateway to further progress along the glen. However, I slipped by, using a side door. Initially following a stream, the Allt na Measaroch, I followed a reasonable path up to a bealach at a height of 300m between Ben Dearg and Marsco. I had skirted east of the formidable mountains that culminate in the mighty twin-peaked Bla Bheinn (Blue hill). From the pass, I dropped down into Coire nan Bruadaran, and followed the river of the same name out of the glen to Loch Ainort and the main road.

The bealach below Marsco

I was only on the road for a short distance before I headed into the heather once more to follow a path round Glass Bheinn Mhor into Strath Mor. Below me was the little township of Luib which I had bypassed by coming round the hillside. A good footpath took me through Strath Mor with Beinn na Cro, its grey scree slopes resembling an elephant, on my left and the craggy face of Belig to my right inviting me onwards. It was remote and desolate territory, so I sang a few songs to keep my spirits up as I followed the Strath Mor River where a heron sitting patiently seemed unconcerned by the sound of a goose farting in the fog. At Loch na Sguabaidh, the water level must have risen over the years as parts of the path disappeared into the water. When I reached the road to Elgol I was at the head of yet another sea loch, this time Loch Slappin.

Walking along the road by the shore I camped just past a slipway, setting up my tent in a grassy area, in what looked like the site of an old caravan park. This wasn't strictly the best place to wild camp as there were houses in view whose occupants may have taken offence, but it was after 8pm, and I would be gone without a trace before 8am the following morning.

As usual I was ravenously hungry by the time I stopped. I set up the tent and boiled up the water for my evening meal. Usually this consisted of quick cook pasta or egg noodles, with a pour over sauce. Desert was instant semolina or custard with a cup of black coffee to finish. This was all made quickly with just one litre of boiling water. There were around 1,000 calories in this meal and my daily target intake was 4,000 calories. Breakfast, lunch and dinner were all planned

Luib with Raasay in background

as hot meals and the calorie intake was supplemented by snacks like dried fruit, cereal bars, nuts, chocolate, and of course, oatcakes.

By the time I was fed I was fit for little else and it was too cold to sit and admire the scenery. I retired to my tent and took a few notes. At 9pm someone nearby started using a chainsaw, maybe my presence offended after all. Even the thought of what someone with a chainsaw could do to a guy in a tent struggling to get out of a cocoon-like sleeping bag wasn't enough to prevent me from sleep. After a couple of pages of *Zen and the Art of Motorcycle Maintenance* I was a goner.

I awoke at 6am and packed up my stuff as the sun rose over Loch Slappin. Duly warmed and suitably encouraged, I followed the road along the loch side. It was a beautiful crystal clear morning, the birds were singing and Meg seemed fine with her rucksack back on. Happy days!

The only settlement I came across on the final 8kms of my walk to Elgol was the small hamlet of Kilmarie with its ancient graveyard full of MacKinnons. The road climbed up 100m as it went round Ben Meabost, and then carried on until we met some of the houses on the outskirts of Elgol. At a break in the hills there were stunning views of the Cuillin ridge. From this angle the whole ridge could be seen and as I got closer to the harbour the views just got better. The sky and the sea were a rich cobalt blue, the brown jagged peaks of the ridge in sharp contrast.

Charles had made a single overnight march from Portree to Elgol and must have been exhausted when he arrived. The journey had been made in treacherous conditions and at one point the Prince had sunk into a bog right up to his thighs. At least his companion Malcolm MacLeod was there to pull him out! They ate and rested at Captain John MacKinnon's house, a relation of MacLeod, although the Captain was absent at the time. The housemaid washed MacLeod's legs but took exception to washing the legs of another servant. Eventually MacLeod 'prevailed upon the maid to stoop so far as to wash poor Lewie's feet.' The girl handled the Prince 'roughly' and he cried out 'O MacLeod if you would desire the girl not to go so far up.'

Returning home to find Charles carrying and singing to his infant son, Captain McKinnon turned away to weep as the Prince said 'I hope this child may be a captain in my service yet.'

Later in the day the Prince waited in a cave where he shared a meal with the McKinnon chief and his wife. At dusk he set out for another journey by sea over to Mallaig. There is now little trace of Captain McKinnon's house, so I set out to find the cave. I headed south across the heather to the end of the peninsula at Port an Luig Mhoir.

A secluded, stony beach was littered with washed up plastic, and a few sheep were feeding on the grassy edges. I climbed over rocks in a north-westerly direction until I could go no further. Waiting half an hour, the tide receded enough for me to continue. I told Meg to stay, and I jumped between rocks protruding from the sea as I moved along the shore looking for the cave entrance.

The sandstone cliffs of which I was at the foot were high and I reached Suidhe Biorach (the pointed seat), a high overhanging cliff and a well-known rock climber's haunt. Realising I had gone too far I re-read my directions from www.walkhighlands.co.uk (without which I would have been doomed to failure). Turning back I eventually found my target, and scrambled up the left side of some boulders until I was six metres above the sea floor.

The cave at Elgol

The mouth of the cave was large and sloped inwards making the interior like a large bowl. There was also a long narrow passage at the rear. The cave had excellent views and was well above the high tide mark, an excellent place to hide. Charles enjoyed a meal here but did not stay overnight. Accompanied by the Chief of the MacKinnons, the Prince left here for the trip across the Sound of Sleat to Mallaig. After nine weeks on the run in the Outer and Inner Hebrides, the Prince left them for the final time on 4 July.

Aware that I had left Meg for too long, I descended the rocks and hurried along the shore. However even from a distance I could see she wasn't there... Panicking slightly, I looked about and then upwards, noticing her outline as she perched on the top of a high cliff looking down at me.

I rushed back to the spot where I had left her and began calling her name. She didn't return. I tried unsuccessfully to find a way up the cliff. After retracing my steps back to Port an Luig Mhoir I found a way up. To get to where I thought Meg was entailed me jumping over a chasm, not wide enough to be difficult but enough to give palpitations if you stared too long. With my adrenalin rushing I didn't think twice. I got to the top and Meg came dashing over. Mightily relieved I led her down, this time finding an easier descent.

Meg on the cliff top

Walking back to Elgol, I had a chat with Meg about the dangers of cliffs, crumbling edges and why I couldn't keep changing my pants.

At the local shop, sitting at a picnic table with a cup of coffee and a buttered scone was paradise. I lay back and relaxed in the sunshine. After a strenuous morning, these simple pleasures were so satisfying.

From the car park, the bus left for Broadford, where I would take a further bus to Armadale, and then a ferry to Mallaig. I got talking to Tim who was from York, and was travelling around Scotland. He was waiting for a friend who was arriving on this bus so they could walk to Loch Coruisk together. I asked him if he was aware of the so-called Bad Step. He had heard of it but wasn't sure of any more details. From the route he talked of he was going to have to cross it. He had a big rucksack and was packing a guitar too.

The Bad Step is a large slab of rock dissecting the path between Camasunary and Loch Coruisk. To cross it requires walking along a narrow ledge; fall and you're in the ocean.

However when the bus arrived his friend was nowhere to be seen, so my concerns were immaterial. What did I know anyway? I was acting like a do-gooder, but I just needed to talk. Tim joined me on the bus for Broadford, deciding to go to Portree instead and I started rabbiting on again. Couldn't help myself. Thankfully, he was a good listener, although to be honest he didn't have much option. I went on about things to do in Skye, in Portree, caves, pubs, summits, yah de yah, like a walking tourist information board. When I eventually ran out of steam, we discovered a mutual interest in football, and then I went off on one again. Poor guy. I restocked my provisions at Broadford whilst Tim sat with Meg; both of them probably glad to be rid of this gibbering madman for a while. I went into the Co-op store and gave the cereal boxes a good talking too. At last I said cheerio to Tim and boarded the bus for Armadale, which was full of school kids. Meg went for a wander amongst them and they all took a turn to pat her, whilst ignoring the guy muttering away in his seat.

Getting on my last Caledonian MacBrayne ferry of the trip, I settled down to look at maps of the next stage of my journey, wondering where the emotional outpouring had come from.

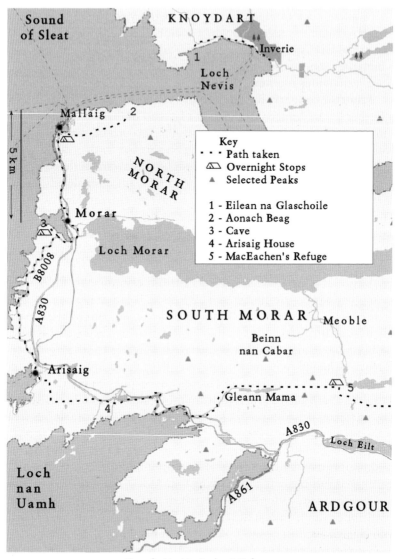

Knoydart to MacEachen's Refuge

CHAPTER 5

Mallaig to Glen Shiel

CROSSING THE SOUND of Sleat, I returned to Mallaig, in high spirits and looking forward to my forthcoming trip to Inverie on the Knoydart Peninsula. I camped up on a soggy hillside behind the village and the following morning I left my tent at 6.30am and headed for the summit of Aonach Beag, three kilometres away.

The Prince stayed in the vicinity of Mallaig, sleeping rough for three days, gaining neither shelter nor support. Impatience got the better of him and he sailed off along Loch Nevis on a reconnaissance mission. His party hadn't travelled very far when they disturbed a party of sentries at Earnsaig, at the head of the Loch. The soldiers launched their own boat to give chase but the Prince's boat did a swift about turn and headed back towards Mallaig. Distancing themselves from the soldiers they landed at Sron Raineach and the Prince climbed to the top of Aonach Beag, where he watched the pursuers return to their base. He then slept for a few hours before returning to the boat, and sailing across Loch Nevis, towards Scottas House on the Knoydart Peninsula.

Ninety minutes after setting off, I too reached the top of Aonach Beag (340m) having crossed pathless, heather covered hillsides where the rocky summit gave commanding views over Loch Nevis below. I returned to my tent, my baggage and breakfast. From my position on the hillside, I could hear the cry of the gulls down at the harbour as well as the sounds of hammering coming from the boat repair yard, announcing the start of the working day.

Heading down to the harbour I sought out my ride to Inverie. Tied up to the pier was my boat, and it resembled a World War II beach landing craft, already loaded with a Land Rover. The only other passenger was Richard, out bagging Munros on his bike. Travelling by train from his home in the south of England to the appropriate rail station, he cycled to the hill foots before engaging his walking boots. Clumsily, I said it was going to take him a while to complete them all,

The *Meri 3*

but I was missing the point. He enjoyed being in the hills and took pleasure in his alternative approach.

The skipper, Drew, chatted away as we awaited leaving time. Suddenly, with a concerned look passing across his face, he blurted out, 'The boat's not moving.' I didn't get it, we were tied to a mooring so surely we shouldn't have been moving anyway? Drew dashed over to untie the mooring, and stormed up the few steps to the bridge and hammered the engine into reverse. Eventually we moved off the bottom and were afloat again. The penny dropped. We had been beached, with the tide going out on us. A few moments longer and we would have been stuck until the tide came back in again.

Crossing the head of Loch Nevis, Drew took the *Meri 3* on a short detour to show me Eilean na Glaschoille, a tiny island off the north shore, which was my next destination. Circular, 15m in diameter and just a few metres high, the tiny island protruded from the water like Neptune's crown.

The whitewashed walls of Knoydart's oldest house, Scottas, gleamed in the sunshine as we cruised by, heading towards Inverie Bay.

The Knoydart peninsula, Britain's last great wilderness, is truly remote, surrounded to the north and south by Loch Hourn and Loch

Scottas House

Nevis respectively. To the west is the sea, and to the east it is separated from the mainland by the mountains of the Barrisdale forest. To add to the sense of isolation there is no public road to the peninsula; to get there you can take the ferry service from Mallaig, or undertake a two-day walk in, over rough terrain. Reaching the bay, in true landing craft style, the bow dropped down and the Land Rover charged ashore, with the troops following close behind – me, Meg and Richard on a bike.

With an unopposed landing, I found myself on Knoydart, a place I had always wanted to visit but had never previously taken the trouble. Its inaccessibility is what it is best known for. The main settlement, Inverie was nearby, but first of all I headed west to set foot on Eilean na Glaschoille. Leaving my rucksack, I marched along a shore hugging tarmac road, passing a school and a few scattered cottages complete with some ancient cars. The 10km road is not connected to the main public road system, and only connects Inverie with the hamlet of Airor to the north-west.

I reached Glaschoille House; the tiny island was located just a short distance from the shore in front of this large holiday home. It was a bit nippy as I changed into my trunks at the stony beach. However I soon forgot about the cold air as I waded through the icy water, feet feeling their way over stones, shells and seaweed. The tide was out so I only had to wade out a few metres to reach the island, the water reaching waist height. Meg watched from the shore. Although a good swimmer she needed a better reason than I could offer to take to the freezing cold water. Climbing carefully onto the sharp rocks, I scrambled up to the grassy top where I picked some bluebells for my girls back home, then without delay returned the way I had come.

The Prince's boat put up at Eilean na Glaschoille, and Charles waited on the island whilst his companion, Captain John MacKinnon, went to Scottas House, to determine if anyone there was willing to help the Prince.

Back on the beach I shook myself dry. This was a role reversal, Meg being the sole possessor of a towel. She carried it and it also doubled as her bed. It was smelly and hairy. I had brought it along for emergency use only. When having a shower at the campsite back in Benbecula, I had patted myself dry with toilet roll rather than use the towel. This took a while and a lot of paper. Looking in the mirror afterwards with tiny bits of paper plastered all over my body, I looked as though I had taken part in some bizarre shaving ritual with a blunt razor. As I left the toilet block I could hear cries from the cubicle 'Who used all the bloody bog roll!'

I walked back towards Inverie, passing close to Scottas House, a beautiful, large, two-storey private residence. This was the same house that MacKinnon visited on behalf of Charles.

Macdonald of Scottas had been killed in the charge at Culloden, but old Clanranald was hiding out at the house, his wife being under arrest back in Benbecula for her part in the Prince's escape. According to John McKinnon's narrative in the *Lyon in Mourning*, after crying out 'What muckle devil has brought him to this county again,' Clanranald said he knew of no one who could help the Prince and recommended McKinnon take Charles to the Isle of Ronay. This was not a realistic option as there was little cover on this small island for the Prince to hide. Quite obviously Clanranald no longer wanted any association with the Prince, so Charles and his little group were forced to turn around and seek help elsewhere.

Back at the pier, I ate my lunch sitting at a bench by a large hand

carved totem pole, created to celebrate ten years of community owner-
ship.

Inverie is a short street of whitewashed cottages on the shore of the
bay. The village is most famous for the Old Forge Inn, which is the first
building you arrive at. It features an award-winning pub and restaurant, offers accommodation, and is a stomping venue for live music. I
stopped for some more food in the pub where food was served all day
and I amused myself by looking at the numerous visitor books. Robert
Louis Stevenson said that to travel hopefully is a better thing than to
arrive. This doesn't apply to the Old Forge Inn. From the comments
of guests it seems that their experience whilst visiting, matched the fun
they had getting here. I had a wander through the village, which also
has a post office, information centre, shop and a tearoom.

Inverie

At the far end of the village was a memorial commemorating the
'Seven Men of Knoydart' who launched an unsuccessful land raid in
1948. They claimed land for crofts but were ultimately unsuccessful.
This disharmony between common man and landowners followed on
from the clearances of the mid-19th century when the last of the people
were brutally evicted from the land by the widow of MacDonnell,
16th Chief of Glengarry. Four hundred people saw their houses pulled
down in front of them and were given no choice but to board the
emigration ship bound for Australia. Those who refused to board the
Sillery were treated inhumanely by the factor of the estate. The factor's
men continually destroyed the desperate shelters that the remaining
people built to try to survive a Highland winter. Young, old, and the
infirm were reduced to sleeping in little more than holes in the ground.

Some publicity was given to their plight but no charges were brought against the estate owner, the factor, or those meant to protect the poor.

I really loved this beautiful little place, surrounded by soaring mountains, peace and tranquillity, and although the history is to be lamented it can't be dwelled upon. At last things have travelled full circle with the establishment of the Knoydart foundation, a community partnership, which owns and runs the 17,000-acre estate.

When the heavens opened I was brought back to the present and I made a dash back to the pier, waiting for the return ferry under the grass roof of the new terminal building. On the journey back I chatted with a local resident about life in Inverie. The community currently has 110 souls, a school role of eight and three houses for the visiting midwife to call on.

Arriving back at Mallaig, the Prince headed for MacDonald of Morar's house at Cross, to seek protection. On my own arrival, a man approached me and asked about Meg's rucksack. I reckoned Meg must have been the first dog to wear a rucksack in the Highlands, such was the attention she was generating. This fellow had been researching doggy rucksacks and was keen to hear my thoughts. I told him that it did the job, stayed on securely, was robust and kept the contents pretty dry. Meg's comments were most relevant however and interpreting for non-canine speakers went something along the lines of 'what the hell are you talking about Gregor? Have you seen my scars?'

The sun appeared again as I took the back road out of Mallaig, the birds were chirping and there was a freshness in the air that comes after rain; all of which reinvigorated me for the final 7km of the day. Soon I met up with the main road, which I followed for a short distance before rejoining another side road, as it passed through Morar, a little village set in the hillside above the River Morar estuary.

The house I was looking for was located at Cross which was marked on my map. At the southern end of the village there was even a footpath taking me to Cross, which seemed unusual but was most welcome. I followed the path to a hilltop and there in front of me was Cross, well *a* cross, a five metre high Christian cross made from iron girders. Misunderstandings aside, the views were spectacular, looking past the village to the estuary and then on to Rhum and Eigg. To the east, Loch Morar and its islands.

Loch Morar

On one of the largest of these islands, Lord Lovat hid from the government, thinking himself safe from incursion, having appropriated all the boats in the area. To capture him the British Navy landed 300 troops at the estuary and the men carried small boats overland. After a three-day search, Lovat was found hidden in the hollow of a tree and taken eventually to London for trial. He was executed in 1747 for his part in the Rising, the last public beheading in Britain. A ruthless power monger throughout his life, he would have taken comfort from the fact that 20 of the spectators watching his execution were killed when a specially erected viewing platform collapsed.

When Charles reached Cross, he found that MacDonald of Morar's house had been burned by government troops. The chief was living in a nearby bothy but sent Charles to a cave to take refuge.

Returning to the road, I followed it until I reached the River Morar, one of the shortest rivers in Scotland. It empties Loch Morar into a picturesque estuary. The beaches here are well known for being absolutely beautiful and they truly are special. White sands, shallow clear blue water, and arriving late afternoon, I had the place to myself.

Walking on the sand, I followed the estuary towards the sea. The cave I was searching for was on the south shore. With the tide coming in, I left the beach and found a meandering footpath which crossed fields, had me clambering over rocks and negotiating thickets of trees. Keeping the shore in sight I made my way towards the location of the cave as shown on my map. I was just about there when I reached a rocky outcrop and could go no further. With cliffs above and the sea below there was no alternative route. I tied Meg to a sapling, dropped my rucksack and began edging along a narrow ledge. Two hands as well as feet were required to move along the near vertical rock face. After a few moments scrambling, I leapt off the wall, onto a section of rocky beach and from there my difficulties were over. In front of me, in the cliff face was the sought after cave. The entrance was around 5m wide and just under 2m high. The interior stretched 13m back and was well above the high tide mark.

Although I didn't have any definitive proof that this was the actual cave Charles used, it would have made an excellent refuge and I was sorry that I would not be able to sleep in it. Returning to Meg and the rucksack, I camped nearby and walked down to the beach again, just in time to see a beautiful sunset.

However I did have a slight problem in relation to eating my rations. I was running low on prongs for my fork. I had started the expedition with a healthy four prong plastic camping fork. I had broken a prong a few days ago and now with the strain being borne by three prongs, I accidentally broke another one. I was a two prong fork man. You cannot balance pasta on a fork with only two prongs

The cave at Morar

and chasing it round the pan trying to stab it was frustrating. Trying to whisk my instant custard was also incredibly difficult. I took a mental note to buy, or steal, a fork at Arisaig the following day. In the morning I was up and away at 8.30am, taking a look back with pride at my invisible camping technique. No footprint here.

When Charles met with MacDonald of Morar the day after being directed to the cave, Morar said he could do nothing to help the Prince in his current situation. At this point McKinnon tells us of Charles' despair. 'Oh God Almighty! Look down upon my circumstances and pity me for I am in a most melancholy situation.'

The Prince decided to go and see Angus MacDonald at Borrodale, hoping that he would not let him down. Morar at least provided his son as a guide, John McKinnon being unfamiliar with the area.

Following the Prince to Borrodale house, I took the coastal road, the B8008. This winding road followed the shoreline, which was interspersed with rocky outcrops, skerries and beautiful beaches, the area being known as the Silver Sands.

Glenancross farm was on my left hand side, and Steve Lord in his book *Walking with Charlie* thought this might be the site of Morar's house. He was informed locally that it used to be referred to as Cross Farm.

I passed the dunes and beach at Camusdarach, one of Britain's best. It was the location for Ben's Beach and many of the other glorious beach scenes in the film Local Hero. I must have seen Bill Forsyth's masterpiece a dozen times or more. The scenery, the comedy and the sheer irresistible force that the land can have on you makes it compulsive viewing. Traigh Beaches are my personal favourite further along the road. Here I have spent many happy days with Nicola and the kids enjoying picnics, searching for creatures in the rock pools, flying kites, fishing, swimming or simply relaxing and enjoying the views over to the Cuillin of Skye. Definitely one of my favourite spots in Scotland.

Just as I was passing the church, as I was entering Arisaig, the church bells began to ring, a glorious welcome to a smashing little village. In the church graveyard, near or within the old church, is buried Alasdair MacMhaighstir Alasdair. Known as the Clanranald Bard, Alasdair was a staunch Jacobite and one of the first to rise for the Prince, going on to become a captain in the army and Charles'

The old church at Arisaig

Gaelic tutor. He was at the Battle of Culloden and thereafter in hiding until 1747 when an Act of Indemnity was passed. In 1751 his poems were published in Edinburgh and subsequently he has become known as one of the leading Gaelic poets of all time.

This excerpt is from 'The Birlinn of Clanranald,' translated by Derick Thomson.

> Sun bursting goldenly
> from its meshing;
> the sky became scorched and gloomy,
> awe-inspiring.
>
> The waves grew dark, thick, dun-bellied,
> angry and sallow
> the sky had every single hue
> you find in tartan...
>
> The ocean then donned completely
> its black grey coat,
> its rough, shaggy sable mantle
> of horrid surging.

I bought some provisions at the centre of the village and sat at a bench overlooking the bay, Loch nan Ceall. Numerous small islands, islets and rocks fill the mouth of this sea loch. The yachts arrive by one of two channels and moor here in the sheltered waters.

After a brief respite I took the road for Rhu, and then turned left to follow the Arisaig canal. Cut from an existing burn this canal was used for floating timber from the steam driven saw mill at Mains Farm. By the burn were some really old trees and there was more woodland ahead, Scots pine, birch, oak and hazel trees. The shaded forest made a pleasant variation from my usual surroundings.

Keeping to the path I was soon at Arisaig House, where I was warmly welcomed once more. Over a coffee, I updated everyone on my progress and having recharged my mobile phone for a bit, I carried on. Again I passed Borrodale House, which the Prince found burned to the ground. He hid in the area for a few days and could see that more and more troops and ships were arriving. It was reported to him that a line of sentry posts had been established between Loch Nevis and Loch Eil. The government seemed to know he was in the area so he moved on to a cave by Loch nan Uamh where he saw the numbers of navy ships increase further. With more troops disembarking from these boats, the noose was tightening about him so he was forced to move again to a more remote and secure shelter called MacEachen's Refuge, on high ground between Loch Beoraid and Loch Eilt.

In deteriorating weather conditions, I headed for this refuge, firstly following the main road towards Glen Mama. The journey along the road was difficult with a strong wind and heavy rain but the weather had been on good form for me generally, so I couldn't complain. Of greater concern was my stomach. I was afflicted with diarrhoea and felt very sick.

In some weird parallel to my own condition, Captain John McKinnon who was captured soon after leaving Charles at Borrodale was questioned on the Prince's health. McKinnon maintained that the Prince was in good health and denied that he was suffering from a 'bloody flux.' Charles *was* in fact suffering from what we now call dysentery and had been for some time, however, McKinnon knew that to admit it would be to encourage Charles' enemies to capture him, believing the Prince would not be in a fit condition to continue moving quickly from place to place.

Entering Glen Mama, I passed by an old farmhouse with the familiar blue reek of a peat fire emanating from the chimney. What I would have given for some respite from the weather and the use of a porcelain toilet! Toiling on regardless, I started to climb a path on a steep hillside, through some oak woodland with the river tumbling downwards beside me. I was a good way along the path before I noticed the wind had blown my rucksack cover off. My good mind-set was being eroded minute by minute. I couldn't afford to lose the cover so I retraced my steps downhill to retrieve it, which I eventually did, finding it wrapped round a bush. I was too relieved to be annoyed and set off up the hillside once more.

By the time I was further into the glen, I really needed to find somewhere to rest, and get out of the wind. The only shelter was an old sheep fank around which some large cattle were grazing so I plodded on, my guts heaving. In front of me was a steep sided valley under the gaze of Beinn nan Cabar, which rises up to the north. The rain stopped but the wind was still driving hard in my face as I walked over some distinctive moraines to reach the first of the two small lochans that fill the floor of this desolate glen. Stepping-stones provided a ford to reach a decent path along the north side of these waters. Upon reaching the

Glen Mama

second lochan I hunkered down beside a corrugated iron boathouse and forced myself to eat some lunch.

At the head of the glen I followed the bed of a stream, the Allt na Creige Baine and ascended a sheltered gully up to a narrow bealach between Creag Bhan and Cruach Thoraraidh. Relieved to be out of the buffeting airstreams, I climbed steeply up to 400m. Once I reached the bealach the wind nearly knocked me off my feet and every step was difficult. A second chase of the day ensued, when my map case was torn from me. Tilting to the hissing wind at an unnatural angle, I plodded onward, and soon I was descending down towards Loch Beoraid with the wind gradually receding.

There were two paths connecting Arieniskill to the south of me with Meoble to the north of me. I found the higher path and continued downwards looking for the lower path by whose side the shelter was located. This path evaded me, but after scrambling around on the steep flanks, I eventually found my goal, MacEachen's refuge. With overhanging cliffs above, it was on the edge of some forest on a steep fissure filled hillside to the west of Loch Beoraid.

More of a large crevice than a cave, it was too open to provide shelter in these tempestuous conditions. I found a sheltered but soggy spot further downhill for my tent. There I realised that my zero footprint camping was a farce. I had left one of my tent poles back at Morar. To add to my misery my map case had ripped in the wind too. Bah humbug.

I found a precarious spot on top of a crag where I could get a signal on my satellite phone and called home. As forever seemed to be the case when I needed to talk, my wife was out gallivanting, so I left a message asking for replacement items. I was meeting a friend in a couple of days so hoped she could get them to him in time.

Then to cap it all, when I went to cook my evening meal, I realised I had forgot to buy a bloody fork!

With loose bowels, lost equipment and rough weather on a lonely hillside a creeping despair came across me. I needed a bit of reassurance, so I patted the dog.

Although there was no reception on my mobile phone I checked to see if it had picked up any texts during the day. Gary had not let me down.

MacEachen's Refuge

'The greatest results in life are usually attained by simple means and the exercise of ordinary qualities. These may for the most part be summed up in these two, common sense and perseverance.'

Maybe Charles knew of this quotation as it was written by Owen Feltham during the century preceding the Rising.

My tent was propped up with sticks, but was in a sheltered spot and although the wind roared along the hillside, it hardly moved. However my pitch was at more of an angle than I had first thought. I kept sliding off my inflatable mattress onto the squelching bog. Squelching sounds were also coming from the inside of my stomach. Pitch-dark trips to the cesspit I had dug earlier were miserable affairs. I slept little.

Learning that he was surrounded by troops, the government forces evidently being aware of him in the Moidart area, Charles decided to aim for a port further to the north, such as Poolewe. The outlook was bleak but the Prince's self-belief was strong. The same self-belief that had brought him thus far. The same self-belief that his family had a divine right to rule. The same self-belief that had taken a small

Highland army as far as Derby, within 150 miles of London. The same strength of belief that his Highlanders could win any battle, even at Culloden.

The Prince had just three companions when he set off to try to break through the cordon that was tightening about him. These included Alexander MacDonald of Glenaladale, who showed an unflinching devotion to the Prince's cause.

One of the first to visit Charles when he arrived at Loch nan Uamh in 1745 on board the French ship *La Doutelle*, Alexander was a Major in the Clanranald regiment, served throughout the campaign and received three wounds at Culloden, not all of which had healed when he received the Prince's call for further assistance. Despite having all his cattle driven off by government troops and a wife and five hungry children to support, he joined Charles once more.

The next morning I knew I had a big day ahead of me and this focused my mind. I forgot about tiredness whilst hoping that my insides would solidify somewhat.

Copying the Prince's route as ever, I climbed directly south from the cave up to the pass leading towards Loch Eilt. From there I headed east and broke through the crags onto the high plateau above Loch Beoraid. I was heading for Glas Charn following ground that was mucky and boggy and I hopped and jumped between heathery tussocks. The weather was mild, dry and although overcast the clouds were well above the height of the plateau. Sheep tracks, deer tracks and for a time a line of old fence posts helped me along otherwise difficult ground. Leading up to the summit at 633m the going at least got progressively drier with more exposed rock to clamber over.

The Prince now turned south-east, descending to a col before the easy climb up to Sgurr a Mhuidhe (562m) to gain information on troop movements in the glen below. There were excellent viewpoints west to Loch nan Uamh and East to Loch Shiel and Loch Eil. Here Charles sent a companion down to Glenfinnan for news and must have felt a terrible gnawing inside as he looked down on the spot where he had raised his standard in front of 1,200 clansmen only 11 months previously. On that occasion an eyewitness MacDonald of Tiendrish said he never saw the Prince look more cheerful. (Maclean, F; *Bonnie Prince Charlie*; Weidenfeld and Nicholson, London; 1988)

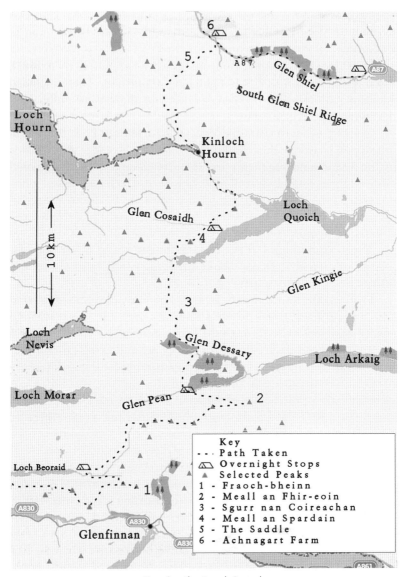

Key

-- Path Taken
⌂ Overnight Stops
▲ Selected Peaks
1 - Fraoch-bheinn
2 - Meall an Fhir-eoin
3 - Sgurr nan Coireachan
4 - Meall an Spardain
5 - The Saddle
6 - Achnagart Farm

Crossing the Rough Bounds

Here on this hilltop on 18 July 1746 the Prince found himself in the most dreadful of situations, completely surrounded by enemy troops intent on his capture and gaining a slice of the £30,000 reward.

From the summit there was a natural chimney that descended the north flank of the hill, offering good protection and a quick descent down to the bealach above the river – Feith a Chatha. After this pass, the climbing was hard-going up to Sidhean Mor (582m). I followed a stream, keeping to the north of the cliffs. Reaching a lochan near the top, I continued east – avoiding more crags – and onto the ridge that led me to Sgurr an Utha (796m). From here an undulating ridge took me to Fraoch-bheinn (Heather hill, 790m).

As Charles rested on this hilltop awaiting Donald Cameron of Glen Pean to guide him and his companions, they learned to their consternation that troops had started ascending the south side of the hill. A sharp exit northwards was made down into Glen Donn. Being pursued by soldiers and in fear of his life Charles probably did not think too much about the steepness of the descent.

I didn't have local knowledge, but I did have the benefit of a map which told me that there were lots of cliffs and precipices to the north of the summit as well as many missing contours on these slopes, proof enough of an incredibly steep descent. Taking a peek over the edge, it was going to take ropes, karabiners and a Sea King helicopter to get me off the edge.

I retraced my steps back to 500m west of Sgurr an Utha, and took time out to decide. Did I cop out and retrace my steps further, or did I try descending north here, where according to the map there was a break in the crags. I went for a look and after a few of moments of descent on grassy slopes I was committed. The slopes were so steep that to try and climb back up was just as daunting as continuing. I took it slowly following a stream, moving away when it became a waterfall and then returning. Without my sticks for support, or in wet weather this descent would have been impossible. Even on a dry day, one slip and it would have been a nasty fall down the hillside. Meg was fine of course; the angle of descent presented no challenge to her.

Reaching Glen Donn, I let out a huge sigh of relief. I had dropped 450m vertically in 750m of horizontal distance and my nerves were frayed. Climbing northwards out of Glenn Donn to get to the next valley looked impossible. The sides of Meall Coire na Saobhaidh were just too steep. I'm not sure even Charles in his desperate situation would have attempted to go over this. Had he done so then surely he would have been spotted by the troops who would by then have reached the peak of Fraoch-bheinn.

I decided to take the only realistic option and head west for Kinlochbeoraid, the head of Loch Beoraid. From there, I could follow the waters of Allt a Choire along the valley to Coire Odhar Mor, a huge bowl of a corrie, which is the next location mentioned in the accounts of the Princes movements at this time. This was no gimme! It turned out to be quite awkward as I followed the Allt a Ghlinne Dhuinn downhill towards where it emptied into the head of Loch Beoraid. Once the adrenalin of my recent descent had worn off, I felt exhausted, the lack of sleep from the previous night having caught up with me. I must have crossed the stream half a dozen times trying to find manageable ground, as the slopes on both banks were exceptionally steep. Fortunately the water was running low, so crossing wasn't too much of a problem, but it was time consuming and frustrating, particularly at the end of a long hard day.

Eventually I made it down to Kinlochbeoraid and started to get excited when I saw what I thought was a bothy. Shelter, comfort, a fire, possibly even company. As I approached the cottage it definitely looked bothy-like. I waded carelessly across the river in a rush to get to it. When I got there, the door was locked, so I knocked. Why, I don't know. Funnily enough there was no reply, so I had a look around and decided it was probably a private shelter for the estate owners. Some desperadoes had broken into a storage area at the side of the cottage and wrecked it and scattered its contents. There was also a bit of corrugated iron roof missing from this section so it was another night under canvas for me.

Deflated and deadbeat I struggled to put up my tent. Trying to make sticks do the job of metal tent poles was just too finicky in my condition. Although the weather was nice and the location dramatic I couldn't have cared less. Once my head hit the pillow (yes, I was packing a pillow) I slept like a baby.

A calling cuckoo woke me early and I broke camp at 7.15am. My insides had behaved themselves during the night so I knew I was past the worst. Instead, as I often did during the journey, I worried about the day ahead. I worried about the first steep climb of the day, the supposed bad weather due and whether my mate, George would meet me as planned at the end of the day? I had never experienced such a wealth of emotions as this; the walk was certainly touching my inner core. These morning worries usually receded quickly once I got into my stride. They were surely a symptom of not being able to talk to anyone, and they built up inside my head. I did talk to Meg about some of my problems and that helped, a cocked head and an attentive ear, enough for me to know that she was listening.

The sun rose in front of me as I marched along a respectable stalkers path following the Allt a Choire towards Coire Odhar Mor. The waters cut deep into this steep gorge with lots of exposed rock on either hillside. Sgurr nan Coireachan (Peak of the corries) at 956m rose up in front of me as I closed in on the head of this giant rounded corrie.

This must have been an intimidating sight to Charles after a day of hard walking. At 11pm, by sheer chance, he had met the guide he had sent for, Donald of Glen Spean, who had sheltered Charles previously, two days after Culloden. The Prince would have been delighted to put himself in the hands of someone who knew the area well and could steer him away from the soldiers closing in around him.

I aimed for the bealach to the west of the summit and started climbing straight up the corrie wall towards it. The slope was sharp but the ground was obliging. Putting my feet on grassy steps within the bed of a dried up stream helped me upwards. At 10.30am I was at the summit, with fantastic views of the mountains, seas and islands of the west coast. Ben Nevis and the Grey Corries were to the south-east. To the north was another Sgurr nan Coireachan, part of tomorrow's itinerary, which was visible amongst a sea of rugged peaks. There were five more high-level mountain ridges to cross before I would reach Glen Shiel where I had planned a full days rest at the Cluanie inn.

Taking the opportunity of mobile phone reception at the summit I called Nicola. I think it did more harm than good however as I felt weakened afterwards realising how much I was missing her and the girls. But at least I had reassured her that I was managing this difficult stage of my walk, and that I was still enjoying the experience. I

Looking east from the summit of Sgurr nan Coireachan

now began the traverse of the South Glen Pean ridge in an easterly direction that would take in four subsidiary tops before reaching the next Munro of Sgurr Thuilm.

The poor weather front I had been warned about just missed me, passing in a southerly direction behind me. A short blast of hailstones was my only suffering. Other than that I made good progress along the wide ridge

I stopped for lunch before the last pull up to Sgurr Thuilm (Peak of the holm), sheltering behind some rocks. A couple of men descended quickly from the summit and I stood up to stop them passing me. After all, I hadn't seen another human being for a couple of days. They were out for a run. 'Out for a run, 3,000ft up. Holy Guacamole, Batman!'

Just after 1pm I was over the summit and descending steeply yet again, this time through patches of snow and rocks as I continued along the ridge in a north-easterly direction.

Charles was led along the ridge to the final top, Meall an Fhir-eoin (581m). Here the little party was able to overlook the Hanoverian's camp at Strathan at the head of Loch Arkaig. At a distance of 3.5km the onlookers were close enough to see what was going on, but with this hill having been searched the previous day, they were safe enough for the time being. Retreating a short distance to Coire Chaisil, they whiled away the daylight hours hidden amongst rocks. In the evening they descended northwards to Glen Pean using the deep corrie to shield them from view.

Leaving my rucksack at the top of the same corrie, I followed Charles to the hilltop. I looked down on Strathan where I could just make out a white house. Satisfied, I returned to my pack and descended down the corrie to the valley floor where I was reunited with Glen Pean bothy, 23 days, 450km and eight islands after our first meeting. I arrived before George, so I hung out my gear to dry in the afternoon sun and sat outside to wait.

Soon I spotted him in the distance, bouncing along the path like a 19th century peddler with his giant rucksack. I was delighted to see him; it seemed so strange to see a familiar face. Whilst George unloaded all the gear, I unloaded all my travails, stresses and worries over the past few days. He got the fire going and heated a salmon kedgeree, one that he had prepared earlier. It was brilliant to savour fresh food. He reassured me that I was doing incredibly well which I needed to hear. I ate up all the details about what was going on at home, pleased to forget about my walk for a while.

Glen Pean Bothy

Washing the pans down by the river at dusk I saw a couple of black shadows running along the hillside behind the bothy. They disappeared into the hollow of a stream, and I awaited their return. Excited and curious, they were too small to be deer and too fast to be sheep. I walked towards the hillside slowly, pensively. Then they emerged at speed, two adult wild boars. Short legs, fat bodies, pointed ears, angular heads leading to big snouts. Straight for the forest they headed. What an unusual and fantastic sight, I hadn't even been even aware that there were wild boars roaming about in Scotland. I ran back to the bothy shouting and bawling about what I'd seen.

We had the cottage all to ourselves until about ten o'clock when Richard from Cannich joined us. Having parked at the head of Loch Arkaig some hours previously, he had got lost coming through the forest in the dark. Richard was on a reconnaissance mission, logging information on birds of prey in the area. He was looking out for golden eagles in particular, and was a fount of all knowledge on all things ornithological. In some of the nearby eagle eyries he had found pine marten bones. He was heading along Glen Pean tomorrow to Oban bothy. I wished him all the best with that! Richard also enlightened me on the wild boar, explaining that boar had been farmed in Glen Dessary, the next glen to the north. Some had escaped around 10–15

Wild boar

years ago and became feral. I found out later that wild boar hunting is now a paid-for activity at Glen Dessary Estate.

Eleven o'clock was a late night for me. George and I retired to the upstairs floor to sleep, leaving Richard to his late tea. Meg kept him company downstairs. Then I found something else to worry about, my right leg developed a nervous twitch and was making involuntary spasms every few seconds. It prevented me from sleeping for some time.

I awoke at 7am the next morning. Through the night the bothy had been colder than the tent. George said that he had woken during the night to the sounds of rustling and had thought that there were rats scurrying around preventing him from getting back to sleep. Latterly he realised that the rustling was coming from my sleeping bag. I told him about my twitch and he accepted this explanation without further comment.

Another glorious day and a bit of company. Happy days. We climbed Meall nan Spardan from directly behind the bothy. It was an unrelenting and consistently steep ascent on grassy slopes, George preferred to go straight up rather than zigzagging, and I was happy to go with the flow. In less than an hour we had climbed 500m to reach the summit ridge. Again, the views were stunning. I was so fortunate to get so much good weather, which allowed me to reap the rewards of my climbing efforts. We descended a shoulder of our hill, George pointing out Meadow Pippets flitting around the slopes. This northern spur deposited us on a good track just west of A Chuil bothy in Glen Dessary. At a small tarn, common sandpipers were walking on the shore. Overhead a flock of geese were heading to their breeding grounds in more northern climes.

Amongst the boggy ground, George identified a couple of small insectivorous plants. Butterwort, with green leaves shaped like a starfish and Sundew with red tentacles. I mention this because they feed on Scotland's Summer Bane. Midges or any other unfortunate insects that land on the leaves or tentacles are stuck fast and the plants envelop them before digesting them.

Was it just a coincidence or was all this wildlife appearing because a wildlife expert was with me? It didn't matter, my eyes were being opened to more of nature's creations and I promised myself I'd

Coire nan Gall

become extra observant in future, and appreciate the natural beauty around me.

Reaching the more northerly track running along this part of Glen Dessary, George and I went our separate ways. He had been a real help, and had boosted my morale at a critical time. George headed back along the path to his car at Strathan and I headed for Sgurr nan Coireachan, a big hill on another east-west ridge that incorporated five Munros. Twisting up a rocky southern spur was a good Munro-baggers path, which I stuck with until I reached 700m. At this point I left the beaten track and contoured round the hill in a westerly direction towards Bealach nan Gall. There were some sheer slopes to traverse but this saved me summiting the hill unnecessarily. This high pass was choked with exposed rock and boulders. I picked my way through a tumble of megalith material as I descended into the shaded corrie on the other side.

The cool clear waters of the descending stream began with a chuckling, then, as I got further down, swelled to a babbling. It finally gushed over stones as tributaries merged together.

I startled a herd of about 50 deer and chased them northwards. Even on my own, this was wildlife I couldn't fail to notice.

As the slopes of Coire nan Gall eased, the ground underfoot became grassy and it became a pleasant downwards stroll. Charles and his companions found no sustenance or signs of life in this large corrie and moved onwards towards Loch Quoich. I sat by the winding river on a beautiful day with stunning scenery all around and I realised once more how much this trip had fulfilled my desire to escape to the hills. This was it, I was doing it, I was more than halfway there and I was truly happy and totally content. Meg? I think she was having the time of her life too. Almost total freedom for days on end. No lead, no hassles, she kept just ahead of me following the trail. Even without a path, she soon picked up the general direction of travel and trotted ahead.

Approaching the western extent of Loch Quoich, I realised more than ever before that I was in remote terrain. To amplify the feeling, I saw my first ever snake in the Highlands, albeit a little one, perhaps 15cm long. I started poking about in the hole that it slithered into to see if I could get another glimpse, but I was fearful of a tap on the shoulder from its mum, so I backed off. Loch Quoich has a man-made dam at its east end, miles from my current location, which has raised the water level 30m and more than doubled the surface area of the water since the Prince's time. Completed in 1962, it submerged, amongst other things, Glenquoich Lodge which was a large rambling sporting retreat, frequented by King Edward VII and the painter Sir Edwin Landseer.

Charles had taken the same route I had just completed to get this far and in the vicinity of the current head of the loch he had rested for the day while soldiers searched all around for him. Although search parties came close by the Prince remained secure until nightfall.

At the head of Loch Quoich, I looked west along the V-shaped valley where the pyramid shape of Knoydart's Luinne Bheinn dominated. It was five o'clock and decision time. Set up camp here in the bright sunshine, lie back and relax, or push on, for one more up and over into Glen Cosaidh? The climb won, I didn't think I could content myself with the hill staring at me all evening. As well as that I still had fire in the belly after a late lunch. I zigzagged up the grassy slopes of Druim Chosaidh.

There were sentries on this ridge that the Prince managed to avoid. Reaching a bealach, I climbed up to Meall an Spardain (640m), the most easterly top on the ridge.

Glen Cosaidh

The north side of the ridge was rocky and I descended in a north-easterly direction between rocky spurs that would have offered plenty of cover to the fugitives as they crept down to Glen Cosaidh. Stopping at a loop in the river on the wide flat valley floor, I lay on the grass happy and tired and enjoyed the last of the evening sunshine before setting up my evening's accommodation.

As the Prince approached this valley floor there were a line of sentries stationed along the glen with fires burning. Slipping by and crossing the river, they started uphill once more.

A lovely sunrise soon banished overnight frost, and I headed north-east up steep (what else?) grassy slopes passing above some ruined homes from the old settlement of Glen Cosaidh. Melting in the heat I made my way up to the summit ridge of Sgurr a Chlaidheimh.

Whilst climbing here, the Prince had a fall and was saved from tumbling down the mountainside by one of his companions. I went quietly northwards into Coire Beithe. I had strayed slightly from W.B. Blaikie's itinerary, although no one is exactly sure where Charles crossed this ridge. Blaikie has the Prince's group travelling along the summit ridge and descending via a corrie further to the north-west, Coire Shubh.

They then made their way to the head of Loch Hourn where they rested during the daylight hours.

Descending amongst a sparse forest of birch trees I arrived at the valley floor where I knelt down and kissed the road. I had rejoined civilisation, briefly! The unclassified single-track road heads off east contouring round the shores of Loch Quoich and Loch Garry before reaching Invergarry. This is in fact the nearest village and is over 33km away. From where I stood the road ended only a few kilometres in the other direction stopping at the head of Loch Hourn, where there was a little piece of heaven. It was good to walk along a firm surface, feeling the extra power in my step. The road was perfectly quiet, the surrounding terrain still as rugged as hell. The silence was broken only by the tap, tap, tapping of my sticks on the tarmac surface. To the north, Sgurr a Mhaoraich towers above this narrow pass. At its feet were a couple of lochans, shining in the sun, and a perfect spot for fishing under the cloudless periwinkle sky. At the second lochan was a ruin, Coireshubh, which denotes the old eastern boundary of Knoydart. The narrow road descended north-west, twisting and turning steeply down towards Kinloch Hourn.

Today, the main reason people visit this remote spot is to park their car and begin the long walk in to Inverie, stopping overnight perhaps at the bothy in Glen Barrisdale. The wondrous Kinloch Hourn Farm B&B and tearoom is another reason to call. Civilised tea and scones, waiter service and conversation in an authentic farm building situated in an incredibly remote and beautiful location. I was only the second customer of the season!

What a contrast with Charles, who was nearing starvation as he holed up just to the north. On discovering that there were two parties of soldiers within cannon shot of his hiding place he set out northwards without a guide on the evening of 21 July. John MacDonald said in his account published in the *Lyon in Mourning*, 'The darkest night ever in my life I travelled.'

Whilst eating what seemed like the best scrambled eggs ever made, I had a chat with Mary, one of the ladies who runs the tearoom. I tried not to seem too desperate to talk. Mary believed that Charles had been romanticised by history and that it was the Highlanders who had taken the final fall for the Stuarts. The common people deserved credit for

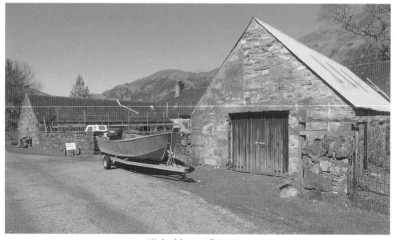

Kinlochhourn Tearoom

the honourable role they played, fighting bravely for Charles, shielding him whilst he was a fugitive, and suffering the consequences thereafter. I agreed. It was a loyalty shown by the Highlanders and Islanders of which we know no like today.

Meg meanwhile was treated to some titbits by the tearoom proprietors as she lay outside in the yard. She wolfed down any food that crossed her path, always ready for more. I was feeding her working dog food, but the amount was strictly rationed. She was now as fit as a fiddle, hardly an ounce of fat on her. Her coat had lightened in the sun to shades of ginger.

Regretfully, I dragged myself away, crossed the Lochourn River flowing into the loch and followed the path towards Corrie Mhalagain. From there I would cross the pass and head northwards into Glen Shiel.

Trying to avoid the lodge house I took the wrong track and ended up in a field, causing the grazing horses to stampede. Maybe they thought Meg was a fox! The correct path ran right past both the lodge and a private dwelling, which was a little uncomfortable, but the signage kept me right.

Next, I got lost in the policies of the aforementioned lodge, and ended up taking an unintended tour of the woodland and gardens. Getting to the stage where I needed a guide myself, finally I found the correct path and walked steeply uphill following a line of electricity pylons which were en-route to the Isle of Skye.

As the path eventually levelled out, I was treated to an amazing spectacle of Loch Hourn. Often called majestic and fjord like, it shimmered lazily, the surrounding hillsides dropping steeply into the water. Behind it, Ladhar Bheinn (Forked mountain) at over 1,000m dominated, with its long south-easterly ridge above Coire Dhorrcail's 300m cliffs.

I crossed Coire Reidh, and forded the river on the higher of two paths, beside a small, strange and isolated shelter. I guess the shooting clients wait here for their transportation. The wide shallow waters were an easy cross, but would be a handful in wet weather, with the corrie funnelling all its tributaries down here. Rounding the footslopes of Sgurr na Sgine (Peak of the knife), I entered Coire Mhalagain where the path ended at the river flowing down from the pass. Across the river to the north was the tapered peak of The Saddle. Making up the southern corrie wall were the precipitous slopes of Sgurr na Sgine. I headed for the bealach between these peaks, finding and following various bits of path that all eventually petered out amongst the undulating scrub. Giving up, I returned to the river's edge and followed its course, the slopes steepening sharply as I approached the pass.

Finally I made it to the top, feeling the effects of my long day in the sun. Above me to the north was the Forcan ridge, a delight for scramblers with pinnacles and sections of knife-edge rock, providing the most exhilarating route for climbing The Saddle. That was no route for Meg, the rucksack, and me but I toyed with the idea of keeping my height and following the slopes round to Meallan Odhar. In the end, I

Coire Mhalagain

decided the scree filled incline looked just a bit too steep and slippery, so I descended from the pass into a second Coire Mhalagain, intending to follow the stream towards Glen Shiel.

The going was good to start with but the valley quickly narrowed. I should have stayed higher up the hillside but I was sucked downwards. Soon I was battling near vertical slopes, trying to follow the course of the entrenched stream. Ending up on the wrong side of the water, I couldn't go lower; it was a straight drop into the burn. I couldn't go higher, the slopes were too treacherous to try and climb out of. I was perched 15m above the stream and could only go forward or back. Squeaky bum time!

Eventually I saw a deer fence ahead. This crossed the stream and ascended both banks for a considerable distance. It looked like a chance to cross to the correct side of the burn. With great difficulty I followed it down to the water. Once there, I realised I could probably climb the almost sheer slopes on the other side, by the fence, but there was no way Meg could. While pondering my next move I poked at the fence where it crossed the river and found that it was loose. I was able to squeeze underneath it and carry on until the angles eased off a little, allowing me to climb up the north bank. Using clumps of heather as handholds I escaped from the defile. I still had to negotiate the deer fence once more, which I almost threw Meg over in my adrenalin fuelled state. Once I found the path coming down from the Forcan ridge, I breathed a mighty sigh of relief as I sauntered down to Glen Shiel. I lifted my head to see the Five Sisters of Kintail, the famously prominent section of a longer ridge and overlooking the north side of Glen Shiel.

On his arrival in the Glen, Charles and his party were able to assuage their hunger somewhat, when they managed to secure some provisions from a man called McKra, at the township of Mhalagain.

I camped by the River Shiel on the floor of the glen, the busy A87 road to the isles within earshot. But it was the howling wind blowing down the glen and buffeting my tent that kept me awake. The following morning before heading towards the Cluanie Inn, I briefly visited Achnagart Farm.

In this vicinity, on the slopes of Sgurr na Ciste Duibhe, is a large boulder under which Charles rested during the daylight hours. The sun was hot, but the Prince would not allow the thirsty party to move from their concealed spot to drink from the river below until night fell. Discovering that there were no French ships in the vicinity of Poolewe, Charles resolved to head for Glen Garry with a new guide, a MacDonald from that glen. This man had been fleeing Government troops who had killed his father only the previous day.

Before travelling far, MacDonald of Glenaladale realised that he had left his purse behind. As it contained all the party's money, he set out with John of Borrodale to recover it. They went to the spot where the purse had been used to pay McKra's son for some milk. There they found the now empty purse, so they returned to the father's house to confront the boy. McKra was enraged and threatened to hang his son from the nearest tree unless he revealed the location of the stolen funds. The son, trembling in fear, retrieved the money from where he had hidden it. Glenaladale and Borrodale duly returned to the place where the Prince awaited, choosing a different route to return by. In doing so they missed a party of redcoats marching along the glen. Had the purse not been lost then the Princes small band would have encountered these soldiers further along the road, in the pass of Glen Shiel, where in all likelihood they would have been captured by the government troops.

With heavy rain and a bracing wind as companions and steep 1,000m mountains glaring down at me from either side, I made my way east along Glen Shiel. The twisting road followed the route of General Wade's military road alongside the river. Where the road switched banks, an older bridge called the 'Bridge of the Spaniards' remains nearby the current bridge.

On the hillsides above, the Battle of Glen Shiel was fought in 1719. A small army of Highlanders and Spanish troops commanded by the Earl of Seaforth, the Earl Marischal of Scotland and a 14-year-old Lord George Murray (yes the same!) were defeated by a government army led by Major General Joseph Wightman.

Britain and Spain were at war and the Spanish decided to take the fighting to the British mainland by trying to restore the Stuarts. The plan was for a rising in the north combined with a landing of Spanish troops in the south-west of England.

A contingent of 300 Spanish marines landed at Loch Alsh and

Scottish Jacobite leaders tried to organise a general rising of the clans. This failed to gather momentum so soon after the 1715 Rising and the cause was set back further when government naval forces captured and destroyed their base, Eilean Donan castle. The fleet intending to invade England was damaged and scattered by a storm and returned to Spain.

With government forces approaching from Inverness, the Jacobite army made a stand across Glen Shiel setting themselves in strong positions on the hillsides. The government army began the battle by shelling the Highlander's positions with grapeshot and then advanced, eventually driving the Highlanders back. The Spanish troops, fighting a rear-guard action, retreated over a hill now called Sgurr nan Spainteach (Hill of the Spanish). After the battle, the Spanish surrendered and the Jacobites disbanded. The Little Rising, as it became known, was over before it had truly begun.

I made some attempts during the day to follow the military way that runs alongside the road. On one occasion I followed it for 1,500m as it ascended the glen but it was so overgrown that I couldn't justify the extra effort required, with the main road just a few metres away.

Glen Shiel

Authenticity went out the window in my exhausted desperation to get to the Cluanie Inn.

Back on the A87, I was entertained by a classic car rally. Porsches, Lamborghinis and Ferraris in a hotch potch of bright colours and Jaguars camouflaged in British Racing Green. The smell of petrol hung heavily in the air as they whizzed by, 30cm from my left hand. Sometimes the drivers would slow down as they passed, and I would hear them accelerating away behind me, the cars growling powerfully as they built up to road going speed again.

The morning continued with the wind blowing in my face and intermittent heavy rain, so I was cock-a-hoop to see a sign ahead for the Cluanie Inn. Expecting it to say that the hotel was one or two miles ahead I skipped along the final section, as it transpired, there were only 400m to go.

By 2pm, I was firmly ensconced in my room, the contents of my rucksack scattered everywhere, wet gear in the drying cupboard and a hot bath waiting. I had completed the roughest section of the walk so far, following Charles at a time when he was in imminent danger of being caught at any time. Managing the last few days had bolstered my confidence. After a good rest I would be ready to carry on undaunted.

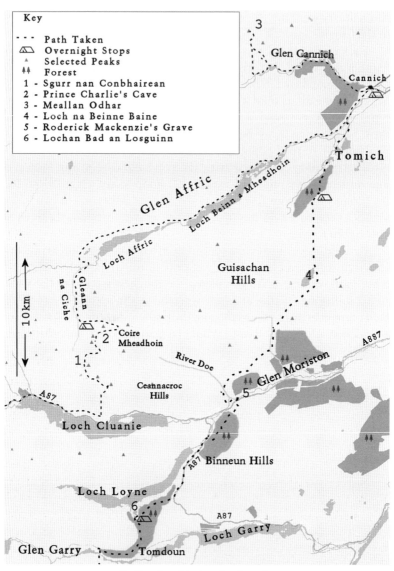

Key
- - - Path Taken
⌂ Overnight Stops
▲ Selected Peaks
♦♦ Forest
1 - Sgurr nan Conbhairean
2 - Prince Charlie's Cave
3 - Meallan Odhar
4 - Loch na Beinne Baine
5 - Roderick Mackenzie's Grave
6 - Lochan Bad an Losguinn

To Glen Cannich then Southwards

CHAPTER 6

To Glen Cannich then Lochiel Country

AFTER A DAY and a half, I was back on the road without feeling a shred of guilt about my comfort levels compared with what the Prince had endured whilst in the vicinity. John MacDonald his companion, tells us that Charles spent the day hiding in midge-infested heather on an adjacent hillside, nearly driven mad by the voracious, biting, maddening beasties. The sound of gunshots told the Prince that soldiers nearby were pacifying his subjects.

The Cluanie Inn had been a pleasure: the food, the company and the comfortable beds. Even a simple thing like settling down at night to choose a DVD, from a choice of hundreds, was a delight. There were resident walkers and climbers with whom I could exercise my underused vocal chords and Meg was made very welcome. The hotel owners even washed my incredibly smelly underwear and shirt – at least they weren't lice ridden, unlike Charles' garments. At all times, the Prince slept in his clothes, plaid, bonnet and wig and changed his shirt only very rarely.

So I recommended my journey completely refreshed. All my kit was organised in my bag and everything was dry. The boiler room in the Cluanie Inn which doubles as the drying room was a furnace. Food stores were replenished with a bag of provisions dropped off by George and I had stocked up the calories internally by polishing off some big tasty meals.

The objective for the day was to find a cave at the head of a hidden glen overlooked by 1,000m mountains. It was here, and not at the Cluanie Inn, that Charles found sanctuary and had his spirits restored.

I started out along Loch Cluanie and just beyond it was the beginning of the South Glen Shiel ridge heading back up Glen Shiel. It had been hidden in the mist when I had arrived nearly two days ago. Now it was a thing of striking beauty, with wisps of early morning cloud still sticking to the summits and a thin outline of snow separating the hills from the bright blue sky.

Leaving the main road I marched along the remains of General

Wade's military road. Taking pride in my increased fitness I stormed up Carn Ghluasaid (957m) on a good path. Whilst taking a rest, I looked down on the tiny cars racing along Loch Cluanie.

'Look at these people down there, they look like ants.'

'They are ants Billy, we haven't taken off yet.'

Some people may think of Keats or WH Murray when on slopes such as these, and I get Billy Connolly springing to mind.

Further up a middle aged walker stopped for a brief chat on his way down. He loved the hills here and his devotion required dedication. After spending a long weekend in the area he faced a mammoth drive back home to Devon. Stopping off overnight at Birmingham he would go home to face the floods that his wife was experiencing. The country's weather seemed topsy-turvy. Here we were basking in sunshine while his partner was up to her knees in water.

I realised that some of the seeds for undertaking this journey were sown when I first climbed these hills ten years ago. I had noticed Prince Charlie's Cave marked on the map and looked down over the cliffs into Coire Mheadhoin and wondered what circumstances brought the Prince to such an inhospitable location and so far, it seemed, from the well-known locations of the Rising and his subsequent escape.

Reaching the flat stony summit, I followed the path over another top, Creag a Chaorainn before descending to a col and a final climb on snow-covered slopes up to Sgurr nan Conbhairean (Peak of the corries). At 1,100m it was the highest climb of my journey so far. I ascended too fast though, and the effort required for kicking steps in the snow and the glare from the bright sunshine reflecting off the surface left me breathless and dizzy. At the top, the views were stupendous in all directions, the silence beautiful. The big cheeses of Scottish mountains were visible, including the Cuillin, the Cairngorms and Ben Nevis.

In the vicinity of this mountaintop, Charles was hiding out, and no doubt his guide knew of the proximity of the seven men of Glenmoriston, hoping to seek help from them. A meeting was duly arranged, and Charles was led to the cave that the men were using as their hideout. After Culloden, these Jacobite soldiers had continued the resistance in their own small way and had scored some victories against the government. Their efforts included hijacking a supply train and shooting a

Sgurr nan Conbhairean

known government informer. They took an oath to protect the Prince but refused the reciprocal offer from Charles and Glenaladale.

In order to reach this cave, which has gained some fame due to its likeness to a grotto, I descended north off the summit to another col. As the slopes started to climb again for Sail Chaorainn (Hill of the rowan), I headed east on a long spur looking for an opportunity to descend north into Coire Mheadhoin my destination.

Quite quickly, I found a section of steep incline that looked possible. Descending the precipitous grassy slopes was dicey but the conditions were in my favour. The amazing weather inspired confidence and the conditions underfoot were dry. Turning towards the head of the corrie, fierce cliffs towered above as I manoeuvred across loose stone and scree, searching large tumbledown boulders to see if they were the clump I was looking for.

It was a torturous and direct route from the summit ridge, but similar to the one that the Glenmoriston men would have taken to bring Charles to the hideout. Huge boulders, the largest of which is over six metres high, form the cave. These boulders were leaning shoulder to shoulder against one another forming enclosed areas where the men sheltered. There was a plaque attached to one of the boulders dedicated to the Seven Men of Glenmoriston, the hosts and protectors of Charles for many days.

The largest area within the cave where the men gathered to cook

Cave of Glen Moriston Men

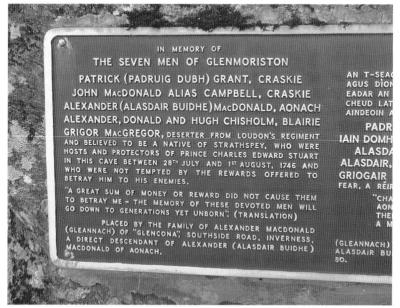

Plaque to men of Glenmoriston

and eat, was reasonably commodious. Patrick Grant, one of the Glenmoriston men, related to Bishop Forbes that Charles desired to be given no special treatment. He helped with the cooking and 'bore up under all his misfortunes with great resolution and cheerfulness, never murmuring or complaining at the hardships and severity of his condition.'

Glenaladale, who also provided a narrative for the *Lyon in Mourning,* interpreted for the Prince as the men spoke only Gaelic. The fare that the expert foragers provided included venison and mutton and Charles, who had been in a poor state upon arriving at the cave, ate and slept better than he had done for many nights.

He would have felt secure here, in the care of survival experts, surrounded by mountains with the cave camouflaged in the rock-splattered hillside. The only realistic approach by a large body of men would be along the glen and any such incursion would be visible for some kilometres. Charles stayed here for four days before moving on. With Poolewe again on his mind, and soldiers in the vicinity, he headed north along with his, now much larger, group of companions.

Security wasn't an issue for me but the variant weather conditions were. It was only 4pm so I decided to make hay whilst the sun shone. I left the cave behind and headed north out of the corrie and round the shoulder of Tigh mor na Seilge before looking for an exit in a westerly direction into Gleann na Ciche. The route I chose was just south of a burn and had I followed the general line of its wanderings, my descent would have been slightly easier. As it was, I headed directly toward the valley floor taking the shortest route, which gave awkward vertiginous slopes to negotiate. Only the extra traction provided by my walking poles prevented me from falling.

I camped beside the river of the glen, and dreamed of the Cluanie Inn, sirloin steak and sticky toffee pudding.

With steep sided behemoths on either side of me east and west, I had experienced an early sunset and on the following morning got a late sunrise. The tent was still frozen stiff as I packed it away at just after 7am but once the sun was up I knew I had cracked the weather for the day.

Looking north I could see where Gleann na Ciche joined with Glen Affric and that already the sun was shining down that treasured valley. Today I would find out how beautiful it really was. On the valley floor was a thick carpet of cotton-wool cloud, soon to be dispersed by the heat of the sun.

From my glen of shadows I walked towards Valhalla and soon the many limbed guardians of the glen emerged from the mist. I was enveloped by swirling moisture but I kept rigidly to the path ignoring the summons of these Entish creatures appearing on either side of me. The chill damp air clung to me; my fingers and toes were ice cold, the air breathing down my neck. Meg continuously disappeared and reappeared in the mist. I felt I was passing into another realm or time.

And then, abruptly, the mist was gone and Glen Affric was revealed to me with golden hillsides, deep green ancient forests and shimmering waters. I had the day to enjoy this and I truly did.

I crossed the river beside Athnamulloch, a cottage owned by the Forestry Commission and used by the Trees for Life group whose work has really improved this end of the glen. On the other side of the water is the wonderfully named Strawberry Cottage owned by An Teallach Mountaineering Club and available for private hire.

After the '15, the chiefs of the many of the local clans were declared forfeit for supporting the Rising. Commissioners were appointed by the government to take control of the lands, with a view to selling them. One loyal hero now stepped forward, a certain Donald Murchison, who collected the rents and sent them to the chiefs in exile. When the commissioners set out to take the estates by force in 1721, they were repulsed here at Athnamulloch by a small highland army led by Donald.

Later that year they tried again and were repulsed once more at the Battle of Coille Bhan. No more attempts were made, and the commis-

Glen Affric ahead

Athnamulloch

sioners gave up, reporting back to the government that they were unable to take possession of the lands. Donald had done well both financially and militarily.

The path branched off to the east at Cnoc Fada, and I reached tranquil little Loch Coulavie with the splendid glen now opening up before me. I hope Charles was honoured with similar weather to enjoy this glorious spectacle. Positive experiences like this enhance fortitude, which in fairness to Charles was a characteristic that he displayed time and time again during his escape.

As if I needed confirmation of what joy I was experiencing, I met Justin Foulkes, a professional travel photographer who had transported himself to this remote spot this early morning to capture some of the glory. Glad to share my experience with someone, we talked about the beautiful surroundings and the stunning light and brightness.

Enveloped by birdsong, I continued amongst the gnarled pines with mountains above me, and mountains below me, reflecting darkly in the dreamy blue waters of Loch Affric.

This area traditionally belonged to the Chisholm clan. The chief, Roderick, was initially forfeited, and then banned from returning to his ancestral lands after his efforts for the Jacobites in the 1715 Rising.

This time around, one of his sons, Roderick Og, had fought and died with his clansmen at Culloden. Another two sons, James and John were captains in the government army. The clan it seems, had learned to insure itself whichever way the pendulum was swinging.

I stopped for lunch between Loch Affric and Loch Beinn a Mheadhoin, enjoying the relative comfort of a picnic table. From the bridge over the River Affric, I looked back along the narrowed loch towards Affric Lodge, built by the First Lord Tweedmouth who purchased the estate in 1854.

Overlooking all was shapely Sgurr na Lapaich (Peak of the bog), under whose dominion I had just passed. From my viewpoint it looked uncannily like an elephant's head, with the trunk stretching down to the shore.

There were no Chisholms around anymore, but I was joined for lunch by a couple of chaffinches, a pink breasted male and a more muted but equally tame female, taking titbits from the table.

At the River Garry car park, as well as picnic tables, there were information boards, leaflets and designated walks. The efficiency of the eco-friendly toilets were wasted on me as I flushed them three times trying to get rid of the brown water before I read the notice explaining that the tank was filled with hill water. Considering I had bared my bum to a lot worse over the course of the trip, I was perhaps being a little pernickety.

The sun was particularly strong after lunch, and Meg and I toiled as we walked along the road following the north shore of Loch Beinn a Mheadhoin. My canine pal had been limping since mid-morning, holding back on her front right drivers paw, and although I couldn't find any physical marks, I carried her pack as a precaution. Back carrying her pack after lunch, she once again captured attention, and we had our pictures taken by a couple of ladies visiting from Newcastle.

To give Meg some respite, I took a break down by the loch side, near some tree covered islands, and threw sticks in the cool water for her to chase. The swim worked a treat and she was restored to her former glory, running ahead, tail up, limp gone.

The Forestry Commission has worked to restore Glenn Affric from the damaging plantations of earlier generations and the success of their work is shown in the fact that the whole area is now a National

Loch Beinn a Mheadhoin

Nature Reserve. The Commission leaflet told me my walk was in the 'glen of countless colours' and on this day it truly was.

By late afternoon I had reached the east end of the loch, where the River Affric begins its descent to Fasnakyle Power Station at Cannich. To begin with, the shallow waters tumbled lazily over a rocky bed, and then at powerful Dog Falls the white crested waters were squeezed into a narrow canyon before dropping into a rocky pool and continuing on to Badger Fall and beyond. I followed the road down to Fasnakyle and then walked along the tarmac to the small village of Cannich where I wimped out and headed for a campsite.

Cannich is the main settlement of Strathglass, which starts at Glen Affric and continues towards Beauly further to the north. At the beginning of the 19th century the Chisholm clan were cleared almost in their entirety from this wide valley, to make way for more profitable sheep. Unlike the more infamous Duke and Duchess of Sutherland, the Chisholm Chiefs didn't even bother to try to resettle their people. They expected them to board the emigration boats leaving for the new world. Even this didn't break the bond that the people felt towards their chief. In 1832, an oath of allegiance was sent by the emigrants, on the coming of age of the 25th Chisholm.

At the campsite I was grateful for the showers, but I arrived too late for any food or drinks. Meg barked every time someone walked near the tent and with people passing until late at night, I was continually awakened. I was failing to derive much benefit from opting for civilisation.

Charles had lodged in a small rough shieling from 2 to 4 August while he awaited the return of two of the party, who had been sent to Poolewe to find out news of any French ships in the vicinity. Eventually unable to wait any longer he ventured north to meet them on their return journey.

The next morning I left all my gear at the campsite and headed for a summit deep in Glen Cannich, the furthest north that the Prince travelled on his entire escape. Quite quickly, I realised I had forgotten my compass and stupidly decided not to go back for it. Although I hadn't used it often on my trip it was to go crazy into the hills without it. At the campsite they had said the weather was to be good until mid-afternoon when rain and cloud would arrive so I convinced myself that I had plenty of time to complete my hill.

For the rest of the outward journey I raced along the glen hardly taking in my surroundings or enjoying the tranquillity of this peaceful valley. My only concern, and soon to be my overriding concern, was to beat the weather, so that I would have clear skies on the hills, hopefully preventing me from getting lost.

Once I was well into the glen the weather started playing tricks on me. The wind blew in clouds that covered the high peaks ahead, then just as quickly, blew them away again. Nine kilometres from the campsite, after intermittent bouts of speed walking and jogging, the peak in front of me, An Soutar, disappeared, and I started to despair. When the clouds cleared once more, I redoubled my efforts to get up my hill, Meall Odhar, as quickly as possible.

I started to ascend, wading through knee high heather heading for the mature stand of pines surrounding the Llatrie burn. From there it was up to the bealach that An Soutar shares with Meall Odhar, and then onto the slopes of the latter, forever watching the summit.

Meall Odhar

Close to the top, I collapsed in the heather, totally puggled, not having taken a break all morning. The fear of inclement weather catching up with me had driven me this far, this fast. Now I had an understanding of how it felt to have to move as swiftly as your legs can carry you over rough terrain, something that Charles had become accustomed to long before reaching this area. Marshalling my energy I made a final push for the top, where the small summit cairn marked the northern tip of my journey.

Here Charles awaited the messengers, who would have been travelling on an old line of communication. The last stage of their journey from Poolewe would have seen these men walking along the north shore of Loch Monar, which I could see intermittently in the distance to the north-west. Crossing Glen Strathfarrar at Inchvuilt, they would have taken to the wooded hillsides heading south-east towards the pass below me.

The messengers duly returned with news that although the French ship had now sailed away, it had deposited two officers who had gone to Cameron of Lochiel's territory to search for Charles. It was resolved to head south and seek out these men.

Achnacarry, Lochiel's home, was over 80km from my current spot. I turned around and began the journey.

Retracing my footsteps down to the glen, this time I took my time to enjoy the walk back along the quiet road following the River Cannich. Near the farm of Muchrachd, I crossed the steel 'action man' bridge and strolled on.

Shortly thereafter, a tractor pulling a trailer filled with bales of hay pulled up beside me. Donald Fraser, the head stalker of the estate, had seen me walking with some purpose up the hillside earlier, and was intrigued. He took a great interest in my walk, speiring me on all aspects. He told me about Charlie's cave in Glen Strathfarrar the next glen to the north. I hadn't visited this hideaway, there being no contemporary references for Charles going so far north, although local tradition places him there.

The Union flag was flying at a cottage in the glen, maybe in response to the Hammer and Sickle I had seen waving cheerfully in the wind earlier on. However the Union flag had once spelt terror for the inhabitants of this glen, as it did for any other during the government's attempt at pacification in the summer of 1746.

When troops were spotted coming up the glen, people working in the fields fled to the hills. As John Prebble relates in *Culloden,* one woman left her small child alone for a moment only to watch in horror as a soldier entered the house and came out with the baby skewered on his bayonet.

Arriving back at the campsite by mid-afternoon, I had a civilised late lunch then collected my belongings. After restocking with some provisions at the local shop I headed south, crossing the River Affric at Fasnakyle.

I passed through the historic village of Tomich, the last settlement I would see for a few days. It was a pretty little village, built by the aforementioned Lord Tweedmouth to re-house his tenants. Their crofts were in sight of the new estate house he had built at Guisachan, which rather spoiled the view.

Entering the woods at the end of the village I began by following an official right of way towards Glen Moriston. The zigzag path uphill through the woods was a treat, with shafts of sunlight filtering through the giant trees whose feathered lodgers were singing cheerfully. The stillness and warmth of the forest induced a feeling of relaxation, and a tendency to linger, soaking in the atmosphere.

I camped at the edge of the woods; my company tonight was *The Colossus of Maroussi* by Henry Miller. I had chosen this book as an escape from my present day job but although I was drawn into 1930s Greece, my mind flitted constantly to images of civil disturbance and then to the debt crisis, banks, recessions and reality, a place I was not yet ready to return to.

The soft pitter-patter of snowflakes on my tent at 6am awoke me from deep slumber. I retreated further into the woods for a more sheltered breakfast. The snow didn't last but it remained bitterly cold on the open hillside as I climbed gently on easy-going dirt roads, newly constructed to service the electricity pylons. There were even signs informing me 'Mobile Phone Reception Available Here.' I fired off a few texts and received a batch of inspirational messages including,

'The block of granite which was an obstacle in the pathway of the weak, becomes a stepping stone in the pathway of the strong.' No prizes for guessing who sent that one! The originator was our very own Thomas Carlyle (1795–1881).

Reaching Loch na Beinne Baine at a height of 500m, the ground sloped away to the south, opening up the territory before me. I left the dirt roads to make my way round a peat bog towards a subsidiary top of Beinn Bhan. Meg, fairy dog of the highlands, coped with ease, her saddlebag rising up like two blue wings as she jumped from hag to hag. The danger for me was not paying attention to my own footwork, whilst jealously watching her sailing across this broken ground with consummate ease.

Continuing on undulating and open moorland I reached the northwest corner of a large area of forest around Loch Cuileig. Here the deer had burst through a gate, and their footprints were everywhere, no doubt having a ball amongst the juicy saplings.

On a vague path, I began following the edge of the forest southwards and then deviated west as there were no crossings over the River Moriston ahead. Crossing a stream by a small dam I was grateful for the good paths created by the hydroelectric works as I headed towards the bridge at Ceannacroc. A feeling of lethargy had been growing in me for the past couple of hours and it began to overwhelm me. Despite taking numerous rests and extra intakes of food, I slipped into a semiconscious state, my eyes merely slits, my mind almost on shut down. In this manner, I shuffled along.

Before crossing the River Moriston I first had to cross the River Doe. My intention was to use a footbridge north of Ceannacroc Lodge. On arrival, I found it had degenerated down to a couple of rusted iron girders a few feet apart. This was not a feat to be attempted by one drowsy man and his dog, however, much of the river water was removed farther upstream by the hydroelectric works so fording was easy.

I passed by Ceannacroc estate with Glen Moriston ahead. This area suffered particularly badly after Culloden. After the battle, 69 survivors from Glen Moriston and 12 of Glen Urquhart went to see the Laird of Grant for advice on what to do. The Laird himself had not rebelled and told them if they marched to Inverness with him, he would ensure that no harm came to them. The trusting men were led in front of the Duke of Cumberland who promptly imprisoned them, packed them off to English prison ships and then on to the plantations of Barbados. Within three years only 18 of the 81 were alive. Government militia or soldiers then raided Glen Moriston time and time again. The first raiders were MacLeods and MacDonalds from Skye, commanded by none other than Sir Alexander MacDonald of Sleat.

Bridge above Ceannacroc

Soon after, another Scot came to finish the job, this time a brutal lowlander. Major Lockhart marched up the defenceless glen with 180 men. Again, Prebble relates how they murdered young and old, destroyed houses and drove off cattle. Near to where I was now standing, where the River Moriston met the Doe, five soldiers raped Isabel MacDonald, while her husband could only look on helplessly from the hillside.

How the Prince coped with all the guilt he must have carried for the sheer hell he had unleashed upon the Highlanders is hard to comprehend. His own desperate circumstances paled into insignificance compared to what was going on around him.

And the Duke of Cumberland, whither his conscience? Ultimately, he was prepared to sacrifice this generation of Highlanders to remove the warlike footing that persisted in the Highlands, and thus secure the dynasty of his family.

I crossed the River Moriston using the lovely Ceannacroc Bridge built by Thomas Telford around 1810. This bridge was retired in the 1980s along with an old section of the A887 road that I followed, to pay my respects at the grave of Roderick Mackenzie.

With an uncanny likeness to the Bonnie Prince, Roderick played a significant part in Charles' eventual escape. An Edinburgh merchant, Roderick joined the Prince's army and fought at Culloden as part of Lord Elcho's cavalry troop.

In August 1746, redcoats in Glen Moriston cornered him, whether by accident or design is not agreed upon. Roderick drew his sword to defend himself, and was shot by the government troops. As he died, he said, 'You have killed your Prince.'

The soldiers eager for their reward decapitated the body and the head was sent to Fort Augustus for official identification. None of the Jacobites there ensconced were prepared to identify the head, but nonetheless it was paraded through Inverness, Stirling and Edinburgh before being taken to London. Prince Charles' valet, a prisoner by this time, was unable to identify the head due to decomposition. By then the government had realised its mistake, but the delay had allowed Charles time to escape from the area, and for a while thereafter had taken the heat out of the search.

A cairn by the current A887 road marks the spot where Roderick

Roderick Mackenzie's grave

fell and his burial place is by the 'stream of the merchant' across the road. A serene spot by the river, to the west was Coire Mheadhoin where the Prince may have been hiding at the time of Roderick's death.

There was nowhere to re-supply in this area, so whilst at the Cluanie Inn I had borrowed a car to drive here and plant a bag of provisions that would see me through a couple of days.

I sat at a bench near the grave overlooking the river. A comfortable place for lunch, and a beautiful spot for quiet contemplation. After a long break I felt much better, and continued in a south-westerly direction towards Lochiel's country, to find those pesky French officers. Leaving the A887 as quickly as possible, I walked through a harvested wood, Coille Ghormaig.

Reaching an area of mature plantation, the next path I wanted didn't join up on the map with the path I was on, and I had visions of trying to fight an impossible battle crossing a forestry plantation with the trees only a few feet apart. However in reality the path network did connect, it was my map that was out of date, so I continued on my merry way, emerging onto the A87 where it crossed the River Loyne. From there it was a long uphill walk on an extremely busy section of the main road linking Fort William and the Isle of Skye.

Halfway up the hill I stopped at a lay-by overlooking Loch Loyne. A cairn here marks the location of another loss of life, that of Willie MacRae, a prominent Scots lawyer and senior member of the Scottish National Party. On 6 April 1985 Willie was found in his car, which had left the road and crossed a stretch of moor before coming to rest across a burn. Discovered by passers-by, but quickly thereafter attended by a doctor, Willie was unconscious and had blood on his temple. Some hours later whilst in hospital, Willie was found to have a bullet wound in his head. A gun was subsequently found in the burn at the accident location. Willie's life support machine was switched off due to severe brain damage and weak vital signs.

A verdict of suicide was recorded but friends and supporters have long argued for an official enquiry into his death, there being, they say, circumstances that do not add up. He had been working to prevent nuclear waste from Dounreay waste processing facility being dumped in the sea off the Scottish Coast and had taken to carrying documents on his person after his home was broken into. After his death, his office was broken into, and papers were stolen. His friend Mary Johnston said he had told her 'he had found something they couldn't wriggle out of.' and in the weeks leading up to his death Willie was followed by a private investigator who later claimed to have been paid to undertake the task. At the scene of the accident, papers were found some distance from his car and the gun had no fingerprints on it, despite Willie not wearing gloves.

The authorities said that Willie had suffered from depression and was battling alcoholism. An outstanding drink driving charge could also have put him in prison. Willie's supporters have never been satisfied with the investigations, and as recently as 2010 the leader of Highland Council wrote to the Lord Advocate asking her to release the full facts of the case.

I continued uphill on the road, and at its summit I headed west on more forestry paths towards Lochan Bad an Losguinn where I ran out of steam. I camped behind a tiny hillock out of the freezing wind. Unfortunately the ground underfoot was soggy and far from ideal for camping, but I didn't have the energy to take another step.

Rising on another beautiful day, the weather was definitely my 12th man. Whilst I stirred the porridge in my open-air kitchen, I listened to the background music of bird song and cuckoos calling. Looking over the loch, there was just a breath of wind rippling the surface.

I started on what was marked on my map as more forestry track. It turned out to be a tarmac road, a little overgrown, but still in remarkably good condition considering it has been virtually unused for over 50 years.

This older 'road to the isles' was replaced by a new route further east when the Glengarry Hydro Electric Scheme resulted in the water levels in Glen Loyne being raised. Just to the north a section of this old road delves straight into Loch Loyne, reappearing on the north shore, joining the current main road by the Cluanie Inn.

This old road was a fascinating section of walk, hemmed in as I was by dense greenery, with just occasional glimpses of the surrounding mountains. Here on this remote stretch I was quite surprised to see

The old 'road to the isles'

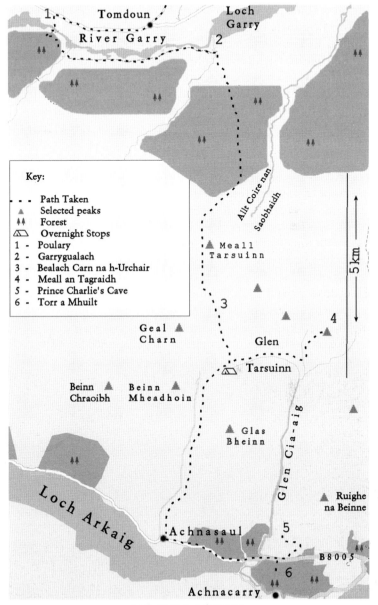

Key:
- - - Path Taken
▲ Selected peaks
♠♠ Forest
◬ Overnight Stops
1 - Poulary
2 - Garrygualach
3 - Bealach Carn na h-Urchair
4 - Meall an Tagraidh
5 - Prince Charlie's Cave
6 - Torr a Mhuilt

Loch Garry to Achnacarry

someone striding purposefully towards me. I hadn't exercised my vocal chords for a couple of days so he wasn't getting away. Rob Woodall explained he was out bagging Trig Points, of which there was one on either side of Loch Loyne. Throughout the United Kingdom over 6,100 of these 1.2m high, concrete columns remain, situated on the highest ground in any given area. Before the days of satellite mapping they were used by the Ordnance Survey to help create grid references for map making and Rob was attempting to be the first to visit them all.

Continuing south I rejoined the road system at Tomdoun, where there were a few homes, a church and a hotel. I headed to the hotel in the hope of morning coffee and possibly a newspaper. However my plans came to naught. The hotel had recently closed down.

The next feature to negotiate was the River Garry, which Charles forded with some difficulty at Garrygualach, where the water came up to waist height. I headed for the nearest bridge at Poulary.

Having crossed the river, I passed through an area of forest before fording a tributary, the Allt Choire a Bhalachain. This was easy enough due to the recent dry conditions, but when the water is in spate conditions there is a bridge further upstream.

I picked up the path once more at an abandoned farmstead. Glen

Glen Garry

Garry was brutally emptied during the 19th century, the houses were pulled down in front of the watching, despairing tenants. The people were put aboard a ship for Canada, with no choice in the matter. It's not simply the numbers involved that makes you bristle, it's the individual stories of the everyday people that make you despair. The chiefs' abuse of their hereditary roles as leaders of their people evokes anger and loathing for their insensitivity.

In many of Scotland's wilderness places a thought should be spared for the vanquished, the people but a memory in the landscape. Of the cleared township of Hallaig on Raasay, Sorley Maclean wrote:

> They are still in Hallaig,
> MacLeans and MacLeods,
> all who were there in the time of Mac Gille Chaluim:
> the dead have been seen alive.
> The men lying on the green
> at the end of every house that was,
> the girls a wood of birches,
> straight their backs, bent their heads.

The river meandered along the strath, the beauty tarnished by remembrance of the departed.

At Garrygualach, straddling a forceful tributary of Loch Garry was a collection of old, mainly disused cottages. The wooden bridge over a tributary looked very unstable, but Meg was over before I could stop her. I had no option but to follow, so I tiptoed gingerly over, every creak giving me palpitations. On the other side of the stream were discarded signs saying the bridge was in a dangerous condition and not to be used. Too late mate!

I headed south, looking for the path through the forestry plantation. However harvesting operations had come and gone, leaving the area like a nuclear blast site, and the overgrown track was only just visible amongst the broken trees, stumps and discarded log piles. Higher up the hillside the trees returned, a plantation of saplings followed by a mature plantation. From a short section of landrover track I struggled to find where the next section of footpath branched off. After searching back and forth I realised new deer fence had been

Garrygualach Bridge

planted right on top of the old path leaving just a narrow corridor between the fence and the claustrophobic plantation. Walking along the gap I had to clamber over or squeeze under fallen trees that had toppled onto the fence. Sometimes a fallen tree blocked my way; this meant climbing over the part-mangled fence to get round the obstacle and having to climb back again to regain the path. Give me Mirkwood forest and its bulbous eyes any day, rather than these horrendous plantations. An old wooden bridge over the Allt Doir an Damh was in even worse condition than the previous bridge but I stopped Meg in time and we forded easily. The woods now ascended the hillside towards Meall Doir an Daimh (578m). Half way up the hill I left the forest behind, and with a sigh of relief I continued on a good path winding its way up the open hillside.

Continuing past the summit I descended down to a col where I stopped to film an approaching Sea King helicopter. The pilot however was not out to provide me with a close up, unlike the other day when I had captured a sequence looking down on a fighter jet as it sped along Glen Cluanie. Instead I turned my camera, to capture the views to the north, looking over the territory I had covered over the previous five days. Whilst looking at the display screen, I saw Meg whiz past, chasing a deer, her saddle bags looking once more like wings as she leaped over the boggy ground just a few metres behind the fleeing deer. I shouted for her to stop but the deer and her disappeared over the edge of the hill. A second deer then trotted past my lens completely uncon- cerned for the fate of its friend. I was now screaming like a madman for Meg to return. After a couple of moments, and with my voice now hoarse from the expulsion of minor expletives, she appeared from over the edge of the hill, limping awkwardly. The rucksack straps had come loose and then entwined themselves round her undercarriage. As she hopped towards me with a sheepish look on her face, I was still video- ing, and thinking about dooking the dog in a bog. Then I realised this might just be a great You Tube video, one to rival Fenton the dog and his exasperated, rather useless owner.

Feeling really pleased with myself, I continued over Meall Tarsuinn at 660m, and then descended once more before climbing up a corrie wall to Bealach Carn na h-Urchaire (650m), the pass to Achnasaul and Loch Arkaig. A sudden adrenalin rush had me moving swiftly down- hill, leaping between rocks, and over bogs, down to the Allt Dubh. It was only 4.30pm so with spirits still high thinking about my funny video, I dumped my bags and headed east along Glen Tarsuinn (Cross- wise Glen) to reach Meall an Tagraidh.

Charles had climbed this hill after walking up Glen Cia-aig but the path through that glen was closed to me due to Forestry Commission works. I had previously written to the head of operations in the area explaining my walk, but I was refused permission due to on-going tree felling.

A gentle descent along by the River Tarsuinn followed, and then a rigorous ascent up southern slopes, heading first for Bealach an Easain before making for the top.

Charles had retreated here from the woods at the east end of Loch Arkaig when soldiers had swept through looking for him. With clear views of the surrounding territory Charles and his companions would have reassured themselves from here that they were not followed.

From my highest peak of the day at 761m, a quick 400m drop in height brought me back down to the valley floor, and now on auto- pilot I retraced my steps to hook up with my rucksack. Pleased with my achievements for the day, I was brought back down to earth with a bump shortly thereafter. Having written my notes up as usual after my dinner, I thought I'd watch my video and revel in the You Tube fame I was going to find. Replaying the footage I was horrified to find that I had only a one second shot of a distant helicopter! I couldn't believe it, there must be a file somewhere on the camera with Meg, the deer and me. But no, it wasn't there. The camera had a quick record function and I must've pressed it twice in my haste, starting then stopping the filming. Aaaargh!

With no birds to wake me I slept longer than usual. Eating breakfast in this remote spot at the head of two glens with the morning sun beaming down, I began to see the funny side of my video nasty experience. On a good path I tramped down the valley of the Allt Dubh stream in high spirits once again, singing rude little ditties. Snowcapped Ben Nevis was in the distance and soon Loch Arkaig revealed almost its entire length, one of the best views of my entire walk. Rich brown hillsides, deep green forest and the azure sky reflected in the long narrow waters curving away from me towards Sgurr na Ciche (Peak of the breast) away in the distance.

My freedom was a selfish pleasure. When I started the journey, I was worried about not finishing; now I was worried that I would finish and all this would come to an end.

I reached the farm of Achnasaul. It was in this vicinity that some more supporters, the most prominent of whom was MacDonnell of Lochgarry, joined the Prince. A member of the Prince's Council, he had been present for all of the campaign and had led the Glengarry MacDonnells when the young chief was killed after the Battle of Falkirk. These Glengarry MacDonnells had provided the largest fighting force from any of the clans during the '45.

Walking east along Loch Arkaigside I was on the same road as I had walked on Easter Sunday some 30 days previously. Passing the foot of the loch, I reached the Dark Mile once more.

On the north side of the road, I sneaked along a good forestry road that had been blasted out of the steep hillside of Ruigh na Beinne, to reach another of the Prince's caves. This road was supposed to be closed due to tree felling activities, but I couldn't see any activity. The dangers for the unwary were the giant log filled lorries lumbering past, taking up the whole road. However I wasn't passing up the opportunity to visit this known haunt of the Prince, and I was prepared to dive for cover if any traffic approached.

The cave, situated on a rock-strewn hillside, stands on its own, and is made from two boulders leaning against one another. The space underneath forms a small enclosure under two metres long, less than a metre wide and just over a metre high at its apex. Although a rudimentary shelter its strength was its security. High up on a steep hillside in the midst of thick forest with good views east and west, this cave would be virtually impossible to find, and the loftiness of its position would have provided early warning of approaching troops.

Hidden amongst the crags above the hill was a bag containing seven days supplies, the absolute maximum amount I could carry. But it soon became apparent that transportation was the least of my worries. Little varmints had been in and created blue, white and brown confetti from a combination of my air tight plastic bags and their own droppings. Seven bags of nuts, one packet of oatcakes, some noodles and a map – all scoffed! They had even had a go at Ainsley Harriot's Couscous, brave wee middens that they were. But the big man's packaging kept them at bay.

On the south side of the Mille Dorche is the tree-covered

Cave above the Dark Mile

prominence of Torr a Mhuilt (175m) where the Prince sheltered on the summit. Finding a good path taking me three quarters of the way up the hillock, I squeezed under and through thick banks of rhododendrons to find my way to the top. Crowned by rocks it was a secure hiding place for a short period of time, but this hill would have been small enough to be surrounded by any significant body of troops if the Prince's presence was suspected.

The Reverend John Cameron met up with the Prince at this time and described his appearance in his journal. 'He was then bare-footed, had an old black kilt coat on, a plaid, philabeg and waistcoat, a dirty shirt and a long red beard, a gun in his hand, a pistol and dirk by his side. He was very cheerful and in good health, and, in my opinion, fatter than when he was at Inverness.'

The two sought after French officers were discovered in the area, but Charles was suspicious that they were spies given that they had evaded capture for so long in unfamiliar terrain, so he was introduced to the soldiers as Mr Drummond, friend of the Prince. However they had little of importance to report and the coded messages that they carried were for d'Eguilles, Charles' French envoy and were indecipherable to the Prince. At this time what interested Charles more, as proposed by Lochgarry, was reigniting the Rising. Lochgarry suggested that the first target should be Fort Augustus and he was sent to Cameron of Lochiel and Cluny MacPherson to see if they thought likewise.

Looking down onto the blackened ruins of Achnacarry, Cameron of Lochiel's home, the Prince was surprised by a company of soldiers and only just avoiding them he fled north up Glen Chi-aig to Meall an Tagraidh, my conquest of yesterday afternoon.

When the coast was clear, Charles returned to the ruins of Achnacarry, where there was a great parting of ways. The men of Glenmoriston returned to their own glen and Glenaladale, who had been with Charles through the most torrid of times since the Prince's return from the Isles, also took his leave.

Lochgarry returned with Doctor Cameron, Cameron of Lochiel's brother. Cluny MacPherson and Cameron of Lochiel did not think it a good time to rekindle the Rising, with the government forces in total control of the Highlands. They invited Charles to reside with them among the mountains.

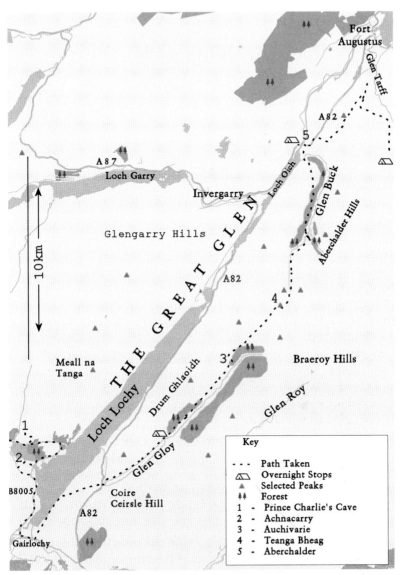

Towards Fort Augustus

CHAPTER 7

To Badenoch

ON 28 AUGUST 1746, Charles set out for the lands of Cluny MacPherson in Badenoch, a wild mountainous region, surrounded by the mountains of Lochaber to the west, the Monadhliath to the north, the Cairngorms to the east and the Drumochter hills to the south. Cluny was in hiding on his own lands, the most famous of his hideouts being Cluny's Cage.

Accompanying the Prince was MacDonnell of Lochgarry and Doctor Cameron, who had served the Prince throughout the campaign and would continue to do so. Cameron's fate was sealed seven years later whilst on a mission to recover monies hidden around Loch Arkaig. He was betrayed and captured, and went down in history as the last Jacobite to be executed.

Instead of heading directly east to Badenoch, Charles' party travelled north to within a couple of miles of Fort Augustus. Maybe Charles wanted to see if Lochgarry's proposal was realistic. Possibly the party wished to avoid the populations in Glen Spean and Glen Roy.

From Clunes, I followed Loch Lochy southwards along the B8005 to the wooded bay of Bunarkaig, where the River Arkaig flows into the Loch. Around the shoreline there were some ancient pine trees that no doubt witnessed the Prince's passing. From here I took a woodland path through Achnacarry Estate to visit The Clan Cameron Museum. Across a field of lambs stood noble grey Achnacarry House, the bold red and yellow Cameron flag taut in the wind. Despite its troubled past it is still the seat of the Chiefs of Clan Cameron.

After updating myself on all things Cameron and familiarising myself once more with the huge part played by the clan in the Rising, I was shown the stand of beech trees on the river bank that Lochiel himself was planting when he heard of the Princes arrival. The seeds were discarded by the riverbank and the mature trees now standing are testament to the fleeting lives of men.

The building which houses the museum was formerly a croft and

Achnacarry House

was burned by government troops in 1746, as was the chief's residence. Of the original Achnacarry house there is little trace. It was recorded as being a wooden house and tradition has it that the only surviving remnants are the remains of a stone chimney located nearby.

Today's Achnacarry House, a two-storey country house in the Scots Baronial style with crenelated walls, and turrets at every corner, was built in 1802 for Cameron of Lochiel's grandson, the 22nd chief, who paid a large sum of money to be restored to his family's seat.

In 1942 the house was turned over to the military for the remainder of World War II, where it became known as Commando Castle. Twenty five thousand men underwent their 12-week basic training here in order to earn the coveted Green Beret. They learned survival and fighting skills and gained a high level of fitness in the arduous terrain.

By the shores of Loch Lochy is a reminder of that training in the form of the concrete base of a mock landing craft, on which the soldiers learned their drills for disembarking, whilst real bullets flew above their heads. These assault landing craft played a crucial role on D-Day, landing troops at Juno, Gold, Sword, Omaha and Utah Beaches.

From the gates of Achnacarry estate I followed the single-track road to Gairlochy and crossed the Caledonian Canal. Completed in 1822 this masterpiece of engineering connects the lochs of the Great Glen – Loch Ness, Loch Oich and Loch Lochy. Thus passage is provided between Inverness and Corpach, a distance of 161km (100 miles), allowing boats to avoid navigating the choppy seas round the north coast of Scotland.

Just over the canal is an area called Mucomir, where in 1689 there was a gathering of the clans to support the ousted Stuarts. John Graham of Claverhouse, more commonly known as Bonnie Dundee, rallied 1,500 men for the Jacobite cause – more than supported Bonnie Prince Charlie at Glenfinnan in 1745. Graham led the Highlanders to a famous victory at Killiecrankie, although he was mortally wounded. The Jacobites were subsequently defeated at the Battle of Dunkeld and the Rising petered out thereafter in Scotland, although it continued in Ireland for another two years.

Mucomir Farm was the home of Alexander Anthony Cameron (1877–1951) a highland games champion and holder of 14 world records in heavyweight events. He toured as far afield as Australia and New Zealand before retiring to the family farm here. Passing through some fields belonging to the farm, I picked up a track following the eastern shore of Loch Lochy and came to a new marina where a large barge was berthed. The exterior was constructed to represent a gigantic rock and looked like something from a Hollywood film set. No prizes for guessing – it was built by an American! The incredible rock was to be powered by the engine of a Land Rover, but when the car drove on, the barge almost tipped over and is currently nothing more than a floating folly.

The path continued through the woods which covered the shoreline and apart from a couple of minor hazards, I made decent progress until I was brought to a halt at the Uisghe Dubh River where the Glengarry Bridge was closed. A footpath followed the river upstream until it met up with the line of the dismantled railway. This section was wide, level, clear and bridged the river. I followed this country motorway, through fields of leaping lambs, until I reached Glenfintaig lodge at the entrance to Glen Gloy (Glen of the gluey substance! – www.clan-cameron.org/cam-ref.html).

The road into Glen Gloy descended to an original Wade bridge

Barge on Loch Lochy

where it crossed the River Gloy and then climbed steeply uphill again before heading further into the glen. Above me, further up the slopes of Drum Ghlaoidh was what looked like a track running straight along the hillside. This is one of a number of such tracks in both this glen and in neighbouring Glen Roy, a natural phenomenon known as Parallel Roads. One of the legends pertaining to their creation is that they were hunting paths created by the Celtic giant, Fingal. Another story goes that they were roads created by Kings of Scotland to access their castle at Inverlochy. As science gradually replaced legend, Charles Darwin was the most prominent proponent of the incorrect theory that they were marine shorelines created when the sea levels were so much higher. Finally in 1840 the correct answer was found. The Parallel Roads are ancient shorelines of lakes created when glaciers blocked the entrance to the glens. The whole glen below the level of the parallel road was at that time under water.

Avoiding the wind and the rain, I camped in a cosy pine forest where Glen Gloy meets Glen Fintaig. Above the sounds of the nearby gurgling stream I swore I could hear lilting music, although as far as I could tell there was no one around for miles. Prevent me from sleep it did not.

Sheltered by the dense trees I slept soundly. In the morning I ventured further into Glen Gloy on a good forest track. The public road and now the forest track follow the route of an old drove road. This was known as the 'Soft road for Hoggs' because it was suitable for young sheep. It was one of the old routes between Speyside and Lochaber and is shown on early 18th century maps

Across the glen, above the river and beside a small stream were the ruins of an old croft known as Alltnaray, meaning 'Adders Burn.' A short time later I reached another disused croft, Auchivarie, which translated means rather less interestingly, 'Field of the Shearing.' I left the forest track and headed up steeps slopes onto the Parallel Road

Although marked as a track on an Ordnance Survey map, the reality is somewhat different. The section I was on turned out to be a deer superhighway, a level corridor below the redundant deer fence and just above the forestry plantations.

At the convergence of three streams, I climbed out of Glen Gloy and towards a high plateau of rolling hilltops. In due course the slopes gave way to more level ground and I made my way over to Teanga Bheag (641m).

My mind wandered to some strange subjects during my walk and none more so than when crossing this high level plateau. I began to salivate at the thought of some of my favourite sweets, now discontinued. Splicer, Cabana, Trio, Texan. These not only tasted great but were also marketed through some memorable advertising campaigns. Were they withdrawn because they were teeth melters or did they contain too many E numbers? Whatever, it gave me a change of song to sing and I crossed the hills belting out 'Trio, Trio, I wanna Trio and I want one now.'

Dragging myself back to reality, my next target was a col between Beinn Bhan and Carn na Larach. Heading straight for the col was impossible, as the ground was broken up with peat hags. I zigzagged my way over, between islands of turf and heather, with occasional leaps into the soft brown mud.

From the col I began my descent down to Aberchalder, a temporary deviation from the trail. By sticking to the grassy banks of a stream as it found its way downhill, I avoided the more difficult heathery slopes. Soon I was nimbly crossing the stream back and forward wherever the ground ahead looked most promising. But pride as they say, comes before a fall, a prediction that proved uncannily accurate as I slipped off a stepping-stone and fell into the icy water. Clambering out in agony, unable to get my rucksack off, I lay on my back like an upturned beetle, wriggling one leg and two arms furiously. Rolling onto my stomach, childlike I put my arm over my face and sobbed loudly, something which, thankfully, you can get away with on these lonely hills.

Still feeling sorry for myself I limped onwards into Glen Buck, and from a distance saw a little stone cottage with a slate roof and bright red soffit boards. I hoped it might be a bothy. As I approached and saw a ladder hanging outside, my heart jumped, the cottage was still in use, surely a good omen. A sign on the door confirmed my hopes. It was a well-furnished bothy complete with a table, a bench, armchairs and a sofa. It couldn't have been better timing. After lunch I sat on a comfortable armchair and rested my bruised knee.

From the bothy, I forded the Calder Burn and hirpled along a good track through birch and hazel woodland and finally down steep slopes to Aberchalder. I was to meet Nicola here and as she approached I had tears in my eyes although I didn't confess that my lachrymose demeanour was due to a sore leg! My caring wife had brought some replacement items, some decent grub and plenty of encouragement.

Glen Buck Bothy

It was a brief reunion and the following day I got back up to the high plateau and walked along the top of Drum Laragan across knee-high heathery tussocks towards Meall a Cholumain which was topped with a communications tower. From here there were great views along the Great Glen and over Loch Ness. I descended on a dirt road towards Fort Augustus.

Charles approached within three kilometres of Fort Augustus and so did I. Once I had a clear view overlooking the village, I turned south and resumed my path towards Cluny MacPherson's hideout in Badenoch, 40km away on the slopes of Ben Alder.

To cross from the Great Glen to Badenoch, the shortest route was the Corrieyairack pass, a high level route through the Monadhliath Mountains. A drove route from the early 17th century, General Wade built a 45km road here in 1731 connecting the fort at Fort Augustus with Dalwhinnie at the head of Loch Ericht. From there another military road went on to Ruthven Barracks. Five hundred soldiers were employed in its construction, the objective being to allow fast movements of troops as part of the government's attempts at civilising the Highlands.

The road features many long straight sections along with zigzag sections on the steep inclines. Some of the original stone bridges remain and it is the longest surviving stretch of Wade road in Scotland – a designated Scheduled Ancient Monument of National Importance.

In 1745 at the outset of the Rising, it was Charles' army that made best use of the speed at which the Wade road allowed an army to travel. The Prince's men reached the summit of the pass to find General 'Copes' government army on the other side, way below. Rather than face the Jacobites, Cope decided to retreat, leaving the way open for Charles to continue south, firstly to Perth and then to Edinburgh. Master of Scotland without having to fight a battle, with surely a tipped hat in appreciation of General Wade.

Steep sided Glen Tilt, with its remnant of ancient woodland was on my left as I ascended this historic route. W.B. Blaikie has Charles coming along the Glen rather than along the road, but there is not enough evidence to determine which route was chosen. I feel that Charles would have once again preferred the speed that the road offered in his desperation to meet up with his greatest friends and supporters, Lochiel and Cluny. MacDonnell of Lochgarry, who travelled with the Prince at this time, said in his narrative that Charles had small parties of men out scouting in all directions. Travelling at night as usual, the party could have slipped into the woodland unobserved if any troops of soldiers had appeared over the summit of the pass.

I took advantage of Blackburn bothy just a few kilometres short of my intended campsite. This bothy was another surprise, surely a planning failure on my part, but it was welcome. A little single-roomed cottage with an aluminium roof, it was tucked away in a hidden meadow just off the track. Retrieving some firewood from the upper reaches of Glen Tilt, I had a warm bright fire but yet again, no one to share it with. Having spent the previous evening in the lively company of my wife, hearing stories of the girls and what they were up to, I stared into the fire and thought how good a husband and father I was going to be when I got home.

Meg's pacing around on the wooden floor woke me and with overpowering thoughts of the big day to come, I made an early start on the gravel road. Curving round the side of Carn Bad na Circe, the government's civiliser then dropped downwards to cross two tributaries of the River Tarff. From there it was a long slog up towards the summit of the pass.

Corrieyairack Road

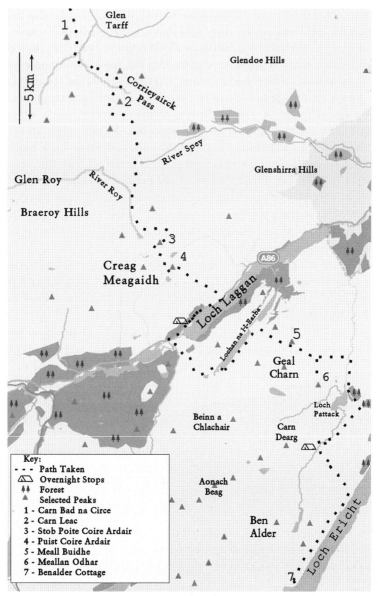

To Badenoch

Charles cut off the road before he reached the top of the pass in case he was seen, but I was contemplating going over the top to make life a bit easier. Impetuosity got the better off me as I rested by the roadside at a height of around 700m, 70m below the summit of the pass. One minute I was resting on a comfortable stone bench and the next I was plunging down a steep slope into Coire Uchdachan. My subconscious had made up my mind for me. Crossing the burn I climbed out the other side of the small corrie and continued under the cliff face of Carn Leac (884m). I contoured round the mountain in an anti-clockwise direction to arrive at the bealach above Coire Cuil.

The weather was still dry but the complex massif of Creag Meagaidh (Bogland crag) was my next big challenge and its snow covered slopes disappeared into the cloud. Charles had crossed this mountain, which from my viewpoint nine kilometres away, looked a formidable barrier.

I delved into Coire Cuil and followed the dug-out course of the stream down the southern slopes of Carn Leac. When it joined up with the Shesgnan Burn I followed that for a short time before heading for the east side of Loch Spey.

Crossing a boggy plateau, the sunken tributaries that flow into the little loch were more numerous than on the map and wider than expected, pushing me further and further west. Eventually I called a halt to my detouring and crossed each one with a running jump and a prayer.

One thing I hadn't considered too much before my walk was the sheer uncertainty created by ploughing my own furrow across moorland, hills and mountains. My experience in walking until the beginning of this trek had always been on well-trodden routes following in the footsteps of other hill walkers and using reputable guidebooks where the difficulties that I faced were always highlighted in advance. Following Charlie's route often meant making my own way and although the map highlighted many of the challenges I would face, the sheer unfamiliarity of the terrain and what may lie around the next corner kept me in a high state of alert.

The weather was deteriorating swiftly as I headed towards the bull nose of Sron Nead, the rocky tip of a winding shoulder of my adversary. I skirted round this and headed south between enveloping arms and into the bosom of the mountain where Loch Roy lay.

Sheltering by some boulders, I packed as much fuel into my early lunch as possible, whilst the intensity of the rain and wind increased. These really were not the conditions in which to continue but it was still early in the day, so I could take my time. For inspiration I repeated to myself Gary's recent text, 'It does not matter how slowly you go so long as you don't stop' (Confucius, *c*.551–478 BC).

Following the course of an entrenched tributary gave me some shelter as I crept up the slopes of Stob Poite Coire Ardair (1,053m). Emerging from the watercourse, snow was falling heavily and the fresh snow on the slopes was slippery. It was a case of putting my head down into the wind and taking it step by step as I ascended the final 150m. Gaining the ridge to the east of the summit I felt a sense of relief, thinking the worst was over. Wrong, oh so wrong!

The C-shaped summit ridge takes in four Munros and encapsulates Coire Ardair with its 300m cliffs. I followed the ridge over the summit and down towards a bealach, the cliff buttresses on the other side of the deep corrie occasionally visible in the swirling snow.

At the bealach known as 'The Window,' a steep path descends into Coire Ardair, which the Prince was reputed to have used. In the atrocious conditions, I couldn't see it and I didn't risk it. The top of the corrie was filled with snow and visibility was down to no more than a few feet. I had no ice axe or crampons to negotiate such steep slopes. One slip would have spelled disaster.

I continued along the ridge, keeping the edge of the corrie in view as I climbed uphill towards Puist Coire Ardair (Peak of the pot of the high corrie, 1,070m). Reaching a plateau area at around 1,050m I became unstuck. The conditions were worse at this height and I was walking in a complete whiteout, the cloud layer and the snow having merged together. I could see nothing but Meg, a few feet in front of me. Sometimes it looked as if she was suspended in mid-air, surrounded by glaring whiteness. The wind was buffeting and deafening whilst the cold was intense. My gloves and boots were soaking wet and my fingers and toes started to freeze. My face was stinging with the swirling snow. Every few moments the cover would be torn from my rucksack and I would have to stop to replace it. It was a world of uncertainty and fear.

I lost control. I don't know what happened but I had a dreadful feeling I was about to walk off the edge of the snow cornice and plunge into Coire Ardair, a drop of hundreds of meters. I looked at my compass and thought I was following the wrong bearing. I took another bearing and got confused as to which end of the compass needle represented north. On reflection that sounds crazy but the conditions were frightening and once I started to panic, reason and rationale went out the window.

I started walking on the new bearing and soon saw my earlier footsteps. This unnerved me further and quite literally I didn't know whether I was coming or going. I needed to stop and take stock but the exposure, the driving wind and the snow made that impossible. Meg had to leap in order to make progress through the snow and I was plain old crapping it. I collapsed onto my knees, frustrated and frightened. This was my backup compass; my main compass had packed in a few weeks prior. I wasn't familiar with it and in my confusion I didn't know if the red or the black end of the needle represented north. I stared at it helplessly, snow whipping round my face. Realising eventually that 'N' was marked in red on the compass wheel, I set another bearing to get me away from these cliffs. Heading away from this corrie, I crossed the plateau and came to the lip of yet another corrie, which I saw just in time. This was Moy Corrie and contained more sheer drops, but I had recovered my nerve enough to keep the cliff edge just in view and head east towards the top of Puist Coire Ardair.

Without pausing, I continued on over the summit for a short distance, desperate to lose height to get out of the worst of the wind and snow. I followed a south-easterly shoulder downwards; a spur called Creag Mhor, which had a line of old, iron fence-posts running along it. Sticking by them, the wind lessened and I passed below the snow line. After 400m of awkward descent, I dropped below the cloud level but soon afterwards the fence posts stopped abruptly above the craggy face of Creag Tharsuinn. More danger, but at least I could see my way out of this whilst far below I could also espy Glen Spean and Loch Laggan. Thank goodness for familiar landmarks.

I swung east to avoid the worst of the cliffs and scrambled downwards amongst steep but small crags, finding a way down towards less dangerous slopes. Previously, negotiating these crags with a heavy pack would have freaked me out, but my strength and balance had improved since the early days. Meg found her own way down; I was so fortunate that I could rely on her. Looking after myself was proving enough of a challenge.

A rejuvenated and natural wooded habitat began to take hold on the hillside as my height decreased. When eventually I reached the A86 that runs along Glen Spean, only the heavy rain kept me from celebrating wildly. That had been bloody rough terrain in ridiculous conditions. I should never have gone onto that ridge. I should have backed off until the weather improved, but waiting out the storm in a tiny tent with a panting and wet dog seemed almost as bad an alternative.

Back on tarmac, I followed the road west, looking for a way into a fenced off conifer plantation where I could escape the rain and spend the night. Near Moy Lodge I came across an old and overgrown lay-by, closed off with concrete blocks. There was access to the woods here beside the river. Under giant pine trees, I set up camp, ate a quick dinner and got out of my soaking wet clothes. By 7pm and dry at last, I retired to the warmth of my sleeping bag, exhausted and shaken. Blackburn bothy and even the Corrieyairack pass seemed such a long time ago.

Putting on the wet gear the following morning was a sair fecht. Cold and sodden clothes sent a shiver up my spine. Warm feet were forced against their will into half frozen socks and then were constricted by bloated boots that felt twice their normal weight. Leaving the shelter of the forest, the weather was grim once more. As well as the rain and wind there was fresh snow on the hills and the upper slopes were shrouded in low cloud.

I walked along the main road towards the bridge over the River Spean at Luiblea farm. I was ahead of schedule and the conditions looked hellish. Had there been a village or even a guesthouse within a reasonable walking distance then I would have opted out. As it was, the nearest village was Roybridge, 15km away, although unbeknownst to me there was a bunkhouse at Tulloch, seven kilometres away, that takes well behaved canine companions. Ahead, a small party of hill walkers crossed the bridge over the Spean, and this finally made my mind up to go for it. Anywhere over that bridge was wilderness territory, if they could do it so could I. Following the crowd I too crossed the river.

This area is an untamed wilderness hemmed in by two fault lines running in a north-east to south-west alignment. Glacial erosion has formed long U-shaped valleys from these fault lines – Loch Laggan and Loch Ericht fill the deep depressions gouged out by the ice.

Between these long deep glens is an area of isolated wildness, high mountains, craggy hillocks and rounded hilltop plateaus. The 1,000m plus peaks of Ben Alder, Beinn Bheoil, Beinn a'Chlachair, Geal Charn and Aonach Beag all reside here, a hillwalker's paradise. The terrain that I was now about to enter is virtually unspoiled by humankind and served only by footpaths and estate tracks.

One such track took me south of Loch Laggan and round the footslopes of Binnein Shuas. As I approached Lochan na Earba good memories of a weekend camping on gorgeous sand at the head of the waters helped take my mind off the appalling weather. The water level was obviously a lot lower then because traces of a sandy beach were non-existent now.

Walking at a good pace on the lochside track warmed me up but I was still really unsure about heading into snow-covered mountains after my experience yesterday. Thinking positively, the slopes were more sedate without sheer drops to fall over if I experienced whiteout conditions once more, and the wind was nowhere near as strong as the previous afternoon.

To reach the inner sanctum of this wilderness area, I had to cross the hills of the Ardverikie forest using the col between Geal Charn (White cairn, 1,049m) and Meall Buidhe (Yellow hill, 863m). Following Charles' probable route, from Lochan na Earba I advanced into Coire a Mhaigh along the Moy Burn. The rain stopped and the cloud seemed to be lifting so I put maximum effort into getting up and over the pass in case the conditions deteriorated once more.

The waters of the burn were a raging torrent so I couldn't follow the footpath over the stream but instead stayed to one side on a slippery muddy bank. As I got higher, soft fresh snow covered the ground and deeper into the corrie I was once more plunged into a world of whiteness. There was no confusion this time. The top of the pass was in sight ahead and I just plodded along, putting my feet in Meg's paw prints, saving me a little energy and keeping my mind occupied as I scaled the final slopes.

Reaching the col at a height of 830m, the cloud was just above me and I headed straight over and down into Coire an Lubhair Mor, the Prince's first overnight stop in the area. I was delighted to have made it without incident and I could see the way down ahead. After falling into a couple of snow filled depressions, I started to make good progress downhill, picking up the footpath again when the snow eventually thinned out.

The path stuck with the Allt Dubh down to the valley floor along which the River Pattack ran. Leaving the path before the ground levelled out I headed up easy slopes to an outlying top off the east side of Geal Charn, called Meallan Odhar. At a height of 615m it overlooked Loch Pattack, which I caught the merest glimpse of before the wind blew in a snow shower that obliterated my view. So far so good, I had done the high bits, so once I was down on the valley floor, there I would remain. My fears had been unfounded, everything had gone well, and the conditions hadn't been a repeat of the previous day's nightmare.

Charles headed for a shieling in the vicinity of this hill. In his book *Bird on a Wing,* John Ure had spotted the remains of a building just to the north of Loch Pattack that met the description of the shieling where Charles was reunited with Cameron of Lochiel and Cluny MacPherson.

Coire an Lubhair Mor

To get there, I retraced my steps downhill, picked up my baggage and followed one of the footpaths along the valley floor. This joined up with a good estate track that bridged the River Pattack and took me towards the grey loch.

I was feeling a bit giddy from my gut bursting efforts to get over the pass but I could live with that. I took some shelter from the blustering wind and rain and had some hot food and drink to try to revitalise myself.

On the north tip of the lochan I found a roofless shieling, less than three metres wide and five metres long. Internally the walls were two metres high. From a distance a grassy mound is all that is visible, as turf has grown over virtually all the walls both externally and internally. The only stone visible was on the inside of the south wall that also disappointingly incorporated a chimney. A shieling in 1746 would probably have had a fire set in the middle of the floor, with the smoke escaping through the thatch of the roof rather than a stone chimney. Nonetheless, at a building in this vicinity Charles was reunited with his great supporter and friend Donald Cameron of Lochiel.

Cameron of Lochiel's support was critical to Charles because

Shieling and Loch Pattack

without it the Rising may never have got off the ground. In July 1745 Charles was newly arrived in Scotland and a sceptical Lochiel went to meet the Prince on board the frigate *Doutelle*, which was anchored in Loch nan Uamh. Until that point everyone had advised the Prince to return to France. The Highland Chiefs were aghast that Charles had landed without military support.

En route to the west coast, Donald met with his brother, John, and was warned not to meet Charles, as the Prince would sway him. John Cameron was proved right and when the Prince chided Lochiel that if he would not support him then he could read about the bold venture in the newspapers, Donald's pride got the better of him. Lochiel's support was the catalyst for others to commit to the cause.

John Cameron of Fassfern never did join the Rising, and even though the Prince stayed at his house at the beginning of the campaign. John was not present. The house at Fassfern remains, one of the few chief's houses that was not burned by Cumberland's troops. In front of the house the Prince picked a white rose, the 'White Cockade', and this has remained a Jacobite symbol ever since.

Donald Cameron was a close aide of the Prince throughout the 1745–46 campaign and was shot in both ankles while leading his clan at Culloden. Carried off the field, he had been in hiding ever since. This was the first time that Charles had seen him since that fateful day. On approaching the bothy, Lochiel and his accomplices had thought Charles and his small group were government militia. They gathered their firepower, which included 12 pistols, and prepared to shoot. Only when Lochiel recognised his other brother, Doctor Cameron, did the penny drop and Donald Cameron hobbled out for an emotional reunion with the Prince.

A few days later Cluny MacPherson, another close friend arrived at the bothy and was reunited with Charles for the first time since prior to Culloden. Once more from the *Lyon in Mourning*, John MacPherson's narrative states that at this time the Prince was 'gay, hearty and in better spirits than it was possible to think he could be.'

From Loch Pattack they moved to another shelter 'Uischilra,' by the Allt a Chaoil-reidhe where they stayed for three days.

Stone gateposts announced the start of the Ben Alder estate and a good all-terrain vehicle track continued down the side of Loch Pattack.

At a junction I followed a footpath towards Culra Bothy located in the approximate position of the Prince's 'Uischilra.' Passing a few wild ponies, I kept a look out for firewood as I approached my destination. Some large chunks of bog pine tempted me, but they were just too cumbersome and too far from the bothy to manage. I forded the wide river, which at its deepest reached my thighs. This was too deep for Meg and I jettisoned my rucksack and went back over to retrieve her. Further along, the river was crossed by a bridge, but I was past swearing and with sodden feet and leaving a trail of river water as I went, I walked the last short distance to the wooden cottage, set on a little plain by the river. There was no source of firewood in the vicinity, but it didn't matter because hallelujah, there was a reeking lum.

I stumbled into a dark but warm room where a couple of men sat round a fire and others were lying on benches. They were a party of Belgian walkers, but I was offered no respite. Taking one look at my weather ravaged, soaking self they ushered me back outside, claiming the room was full and pointing to another doorway. I couldn't believe their hostility. This wasn't a private hotel, but a free-for-all bothy, and I was cold and wet.

Culra Bothy

Through the doorway was a small storage room and then another dormitory room, empty this time. There were benches for sleeping and a fireplace, but no firewood. Here I made home, but without a fire the room was bitterly cold. I unpacked all my gear and hung the tent outside to dry, where it flapped crazily in the wind. Finally I sat round my gas stove warming my hands for a few minutes. I didn't have a lot of gas to spare.

Later on that evening a pick-up truck came along the track and dropped off two men and many planks of wood. It was the bothy supervisors, Grant and Johnny. They were planning a refit of the bothy over the weekend and were much friendlier than the offhand Belgians. I helped them get the stuff inside, selfishly hoping that they might also have some firewood with them, but alas no. They took up residence in the smallest of the bothy's three rooms. Finally a couple of cyclists arrived and came into the dormitory. They looked a bit unsure as they entered the room and dumped their panniers. I had dripping wet stuff hanging everywhere. Once they had breathed in the scented aroma of wet dog fur they promptly lifted their bags and squeezed into the third room with the bothy bosses.

I listened morosely to the sounds of conversation coming from the other rooms and imagined that there was malt whisky being cracked open in the room full of Scots. I didn't give a toss what the Belgians were doing. However, despite my solitary confinement I was happy with my achievements for the day given the conditions and my earlier fragile mental state.

The wind howled throughout the night and the roof rattled. At 5am, the sound of drilling woke me from my sleep. 'Hell, these guys are starting early,' I murmured to myself. 'Give me a bit of consideration. Just because they arrived in a truck, some of us bust a gut to get here.'

At 5.30am I could stand it no longer so I extricated myself with great difficulty from the sleeping bag and stood up. The drilling stopped. Flaming typical. I paced back and forth for a moment to get the stiffness out of my legs, but everything remained quiet so I lay down and climbed back into the sleeping bag. The drilling started again. I turned to look out the window in case someone was taking the mickey. No one there. I tried desperately to get back to sleep but the incessant noise was doing my head in. Then there was a commotion next door from the dratted Belgians. 'This is ridiculous, give me a break.' I got up this time, and went straight to the door having finally cracked. There was going to be war. Meg beat me outside and started barking furiously. There were red deer just a few feet away, some feeding on the grass and some down by the river having a drink. They took a look at Meg and I and trotted slowly off. It dawned on me that the drilling was Meg's warning growl. I collapsed back onto the bench, I was losing the plot.

Charles soon left the 'superlatively bad and smoky' shieling. If only! I left my smokeless cabin and headed south towards Cluny's Cage. Ahead, Ben Alder (Mountain of the rock and water) looked majestic under a beautiful blue sky. What an incredible contrast to the previous few days. Having crossed the river once more, I followed it for a short time before branching off on another path towards Loch Ericht along the eastern flank of Ben Bheoil (Mountain of the mouth). The path petered out and I crossed boggy ground until I reached another stream, the Allt Ton an Eich, the banks of which were grassy and easy going.

I reached Loch Ericht, the southern border of this wilderness area. On the other side of the water were the rolling tops of the Drumochter hills. Following the loch southwards, I met a bracing wind head on as I clung to a narrow footpath with the ever steepening and rocky slopes of Benn Bheoil on my right. Amazingly, considering how remote this location was the path was undergoing upgrading works with collapsed sections being repaired and a drainage channel being dug.

After what seemed like an age, I reached the last section of the footpath that worked its way around a rocky nose jutting out into the loch. The now indistinct path crossed some exposed rock slabs before finally easing off as it headed into Alder Bay, sheltering the beautifully situated Ben Alder Cottage.

Just after the First World War, this cottage was home to a man called Joseph McCook and his family. One winter, Mr McCook took ill with pneumonia. To summon help his daughter walked 16km over a snowy pass to Loch Rannoch and the Bridge of Gaur Post Office. A telegram was sent to the doctor at Laggan Bridge.

To reach the patient, the doctor drove to Dalwhinnie, before walking along the 19km path by Loch Erichtside where he was hampered by gales, snowdrifts and swollen burns. Eleven hours later

Looking back along Loch Ericht

the doctor arrived at the cottage to treat the sick man. Thereafter the doctor collapsed, but was able to return to his car by the same route the following day. McCook recovered and the doctor was awarded the Carnegie Medal for brave conduct.

Internally, this bothy was dingy in comparison to Culra. There were black bags full of rubbish that had been left behind, the furniture was scrap and there was graffiti on the walls. Everything down to the shelves had been burned. I had my lunch and got ready to move on.

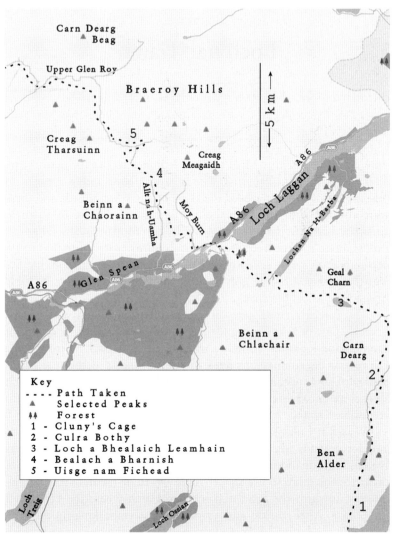

From the Cage to Glen Roy

CHAPTER 8

Loch nan Uamh

ON THE HILLSIDE above Ben Alder cottage, according to the Ordnance Survey, is Prince Charlie's Cave, although no cavern has yet been found. This brae more closely matches the description of the site of Cluny's Cage, a man-made construction where Charles stayed for one week and where Cluny MacPherson continued to live for many years after the Prince had departed. The cage was built within a forest of bushes. A row of logs levelled the slope on the steep hillside and these were covered with soil to make a floor. Branches were intertwined vertically with the naturally growing bushes to make walls. The roof was of moss. A large tree supported the entire construction that could accommodate six or seven people. The smoke from the cooking fire was camouflaged by the grey rock of the hillside making it invisible from even a short distance.

The prince arrived here on 5 September and lived with Cluny, Lochiel, Doctor Cameron and half a dozen others. With plenty of supplies and lookouts posted to warn of any approaching troops, the Prince and his companions lived in relative luxury within the heartland of Cluny's estate. A week later, word was received that French ships were once more off the western coast at Arisaig. Almost immediately Charles made a dash towards them.

Whilst at Culra Bothy, I had been warned that torrential rain and gale force winds were predicted for the following day. My hand was forced and I abandoned plans to stay at the site of Cluny's Cage in order to seek more secure shelter. This was to be the final stage of my journey, towards the head of Loch nan Uamh where the Prince left for France. After 720km and 37 days, I was embarking on the final leg. From the bothy, I followed the path up by the stream to Bealach Breabag at a height of 830m, all the while looking out over the hillside towards the possible site of the cage.

At the pass, I descended grassy slopes to Loch a Bhealaich Bheithe within the Ben Alder massif. Along one side of the loch were corries, cliffs and snow buttresses leading up to the summit ridge of Ben Alder itself, and on the other the gentle scree covered slopes of Benn Bheoil. The Mars and Venus of Scottish mountains, with the loch nestling cosily between. Bealachs at either end provided access to this scooped-out centre. Going round the water's edge, and with the wind at my back I strode along at a fast pace, descending by Bealach Beithe along an excellent path back towards Culra Bothy.

Charles stopped once more at the shieling near Culra, where he rested for the day before continuing onwards at night.

I reached the bothy and over a late lunch chatted to Donald and John, who had cycled in from Dalwhinnie. Intrigued by my taking six weeks off work to undertake this trek, Donald explained about the motivation for change in his own life. He had been stirred to action by a documentary about older people talking about their lives and regrets. Two of the misgivings that struck a chord with Donald were, 'Why did I work so much?' and 'Why didn't I take more risks?' Spurred into positive action he left his job to start a business and become self-employed. Being his own boss, he could manage his working time to suit himself and attempt the things he wanted to achieve in life. This was 20 years ago; he told me he had never looked back.

Loch a Bhealaich Bheithe

Feeling reinvigorated after conversing with someone so confident and fulfilled I left the bothy to head north-west for Glen Spean, where I could find somewhere to sit out the incoming weather front. The estate track led me to Loch Pattack where I took the left hand fork, shortly thereafter fording the Allt Cam. I met a hiker who was scurrying back towards Corrour Station, to get the first train back to Glasgow to avoid the weather. He had a long way to go so we didn't shoot the breeze for long. More talk of storms hastened me on.

As conditions worsened I kept to the lower north path round Loch a' Bhealaich Leamhain which offered more shelter than the southern option which climbed through crags belonging to Beinn a Chlachair. Both tracks met again at the bealach above the loch and from there I headed down towards Lochan na H-Earba. By dusk, I made it back to the bridge at Luiblea Farm and Glen Spean.

I headed along the main road at Glen Spean towards the Moy Burn where I had a bag of provisions hidden. Thankfully they were unharmed and I tucked into oatcakes and peanut butter before seeking more protective shelter than my tent.

The weather was as bad as had been forecast on Sunday 13 May, and I rested up for the entire day. The Lochaber area received 100mm of rain in 24 hours, more than it normally receives in the whole month. Gale force winds added to the mayhem. The caravan where I lodged was cosy and warm and I watched the weather from my shaking shelter, the drumming rain deafening. I repacked my bag, organised my provisions and recuperated. I had been a day and a half ahead of schedule, having pushed on when I could for precisely these circumstances.

Next day with fresh legs I climbed slopes alongside the raging waters of the Moy burn. A stalkers path through the heather made the going easier as I headed north to Lochan na Colliche. The wind and rain were minimal compared with the previous day, but there was more snow on higher hillsides and the sky was filled with dark and threatening cloud. I started across the heathery slopes of Creag na Cailliche, which were streaming with water, 100 newly created burns impeding my progress.

As Charles passed through the glens for a final time, all hailed his endurance and fortitude. Within 100 years the glens would be empty and the culture that protected and nourished him would be destroyed.

Despite the hardship and misery he unwittingly unleashed upon the Highlands, the flame of his romantic endeavour still burns bright as a legendary deed.

To the north was Coire na h-Uamha where there was a pass out of the glen. The river coming down from the head of the corrie was roaring and flowing like a dam had burst further upstream. I discussed the raging torrents with Meg, the only living being in earshot and realised some of my conversations with her would soon have to be curtailed. Talking to the dog about daily events wouldn't wash in polite society.

As I trudged upwards, the snow brushed cliffs of Beinn Chaor-rainn (Mountain of the rowan, 1,052m) were on my left and the more tranquil south-westerly slopes of Creag Meagaidh were on my right. These two Munros met at the bealach that I was trying to reach. The going was treacherously slippery above the snow line. A herd of red deer whom I had inadvertently corralled into the head of the corrie had trampled a path to the pass and I found that the compressed snow of their hoof-prints gave me some traction.

At Bealach a Bharnish (820m) the converging slopes met at a narrow rocky defile. The base of this defile was covered in slabs of snow, which I kept falling though. The slopes on either side were so steep and the snow so deep, that there didn't seem like an easier alternative, so I carefully plodded on. As the pass opened out a large brae extended before me, sloping away northwards to join with the upper reaches of Glen Roy. Descending from the bealach into Coire Buidhe was more treacherous than the ascent, the wet snow a dangerous and slippery hazard. Getting below the snow line, the ground was broken up moorland. I made my way across the dykes of peat to the Uisge nam Fichead, the river that was fed from both this corrie and from the larger corrie to the east on the northern flanks of Creag Meagaidh.

Charles took a few hours rest here without shelter, the conditions would have killed me pretty quickly had I needed to do the same.

Initially, my plan had been to head west into Glen Roy, crossing the River Roy using the bridge at Cranachan. However, at the last minute I found out that this bridge had been washed away, so I was forced now to cross the River Roy much further to the north near the farm of Annat. This diversion meant following the river northwards and there was a path on the opposite bank that descended down to Glen Roy, so I looked for a fording point further upstream. On the way I slipped and fell in one of the tributaries coming down from the corrie. I was able to break my fall so only my arms and legs got soaked, but it was a timely warning before I reached the main stretch of water.

A short distance later I crossed the Uisge nam Fichead at its widest where it looked reasonably shallow. Even so, at one point the force of the water pulled Meg away. I panicked more than she did, she kept swimming until she found her feet and joined me at the other side. On the path, I descended with the deafening river as it passed over large sections of slab rock and a series of waterfalls. An iron bridge over Dog Falls gave spectacular views of the powerful body of water wriggling down a narrow channel spewing up white foam as it went. The rain stopped and the clouds were starting to disperse, at last letting some light through. I changed out of my soaking wet gear. Pints of water were squeezed out of my socks. It felt like I had been through a maelstrom and it was only midday.

The path brought me down to Glen Roy near Annat Farm at the end of the public road. Glen Roy was cleared of Mackintoshes in the early 19th century but remained one of the last enclaves for Gaelic on the mainland where it was spoken until the 1960s.

I crossed firstly the River Roy on a modern bridge and then the River Turret using an 18th century humpback bridge probably built

Looking back towards Bealach a Bharnish

by General Caulfield. This bridge was part of an old military spur road connecting Fort William to Melgarve where it joined up with the main Fort Augustus to Dalwhinnie route.

Once again I was on a section of the 'Soft Road for Hoggs' bearing into Glen Gloy, which may also have been the route of General Caulfield's military road.

Walking along by the River Turret, something fell out of the sky and hit the ground with a thud just in front me and behind Meg, missing her by a metre. She turned round to have a sniff and I rushed forward to see what it was. It was a cuckoo, dead, still warm, but with no obvious sign of injury. The only explanation I can give is that an eagle dropped it. Either that or it had bet its mate that I would never get this far and on seeing me here had died of shock!

I was astounded by how quickly the weather improved. Under a blue sky I sat by the meandering river, enjoying my surroundings whilst my wet clothes lay drying on the bank. Leaving the river I travelled west to follow what started as a narrow glen of the Allt a Chomhlain. The valley widened out as I climbed, where I found bits and pieces of path on grassy slopes to take me up to yet another pass, this time leading me into the head of Glen Gloy.

Descending amongst the trees I soon picked up the forestry road heading down the glen. This final seven kilometres was the easiest going of the day by far, and by dusk I was camped once more amongst the trees at the junction of Glen Gloy and Glen Fintaig.

The next day whilst continuing down Glen Gloy, I met a walker coming in the other direction who was doing a cross Scotland challenge.

Towards the West Coast

Glen Gloy

On the day of the gales he had been up to his chest in water, whilst wading through rapidly expanding rivers. Later, he attempted to sit out the storm under canvas, but the violence of the wind snapped his tent poles and he fled to A'chuil bothy in Glen Dessary to seek sanctuary.

Approaching the A82 at the mouth of Glen Gloy, I climbed steeply uphill to reach a section of General Wade's road that ran along the hillside above the main road. To continue west towards the coast I would cross what was the River Lochy and is now the Caledonian Canal at Gairlochy.

I followed the old road through a forestry plantation and then back down towards the main road where it disappeared underneath the tarmac. Walking on the verge-less A82 was deadly, but after a short distance I reached Stronenaba.

Approaching some enclosed fields containing a mix of caravans, sheds, cages, cars and animals; a man came to challenge me at the entrance gate. He wasn't for letting me pass. He was a dog behaviour-ist and these were his premises. I had to sell him my journey and the dangers of the main road, in order for him to allow me access to his property, through which General Wade's road ran. Even so, had I not had Meg as a companion, I doubt he would have had any sympathy for me. Just as well I had his permission, Dobermans and other fierce breeds were running free, ready to keep intruders at bay. I treaded warily; the boss himself was sporting an injured arm in a sling. The route of the old road became a very marshy path through an area of felled forest plantation until I spilled out onto the B8004 just a short distance from Gairlochy.

The Prince crossed the River Lochy with help from Cameron of Clunes, a leaky boat and a few bottles of brandy. It is said that the later drinking problems stemmed from his time in the Highlands when he came to rely on the bottle. Certainly the brandy is said to have helped with his dysentery as well as providing an escape from the unrelenting stress that he was under.

I had lunch at a picnic bench by the lock gates of the Caledonian Canal that follows the course that the River Lochy used to run. Another hiker, Rod from Edinburgh who was also doing the cross-country challenge, joined me. It was a pleasure to talk away throughout the mealtime, one of the few times that I had done so during the whole trip.

At this meeting of ways I chatted to some Americans doing the Great Glen Way, with Meg as usual being the stimulus for conversation. Everybody seems to have owned or known a border collie at some point in their lives.

What few people realise is the importance of border collies to Highland life. For hundreds of years, cattle were the main export of the Highlands and large herds were driven from as far afield as the Western Isles to the great markets of Central Scotland, the greatest of which was the tryst held at my hometown, Falkirk. Once sold the drovers would be employed to take the cattle on to their final destination, often deep into England.

The tough Highlanders who were employed as drovers were ably assisted by border collies who kept the large herds in order as they were driven along the glens, hills, tracks and roads of Scotland and England. Sometimes the drovers would stay on at their final destination finding work bringing in the harvest. The collies would then be sent home, back to the Highland glens from whence they had first come. They would return on their own and by the same route by which they came, finding food at the same inns at which the drover had passed earlier (Haldane, A; *The Drove Roads of Scotland*; Birlinn, Edinburgh;

2007). These amazing return journeys, hundreds of miles in length, are testament to the intelligence, loyalty, strength and resilience of collies.

Crossing the canal I tramped along the road for a short time and passed some beautiful new houses, built overlooking the loch. Blue bins were out at the end of the drive for collection. With no newsagent within a couple of hours walk, I sneaked up to them and did a bit of raking, keeping a wary eye out for any roving 'Bin Police,' I was pleased as punch to find a recent Sunday Times with the Sports Supplement. Once some of the sticky goo was removed it would be as good as new.

Following the route of the Great Glen Way as it tightly hugged the shoreline of Loch Lochy, I took the private drive to Achnacarry House once more. At the museum, I bought some ice cream and chocolate bars and walked past the chief's house and holiday home steadings onto the south shore track of Loch Arkaig. A lovely walk through mixed woodland alongside Loch Arkaig took me to Inver Mallie bothy.

This large cottage sits on a flat grassy area by the river and had been flooded by the recent downpours. One of the two sitting rooms had dried out and I got a fire going and unpacked all my gear. After reading my stolen newspaper I began to feel lonely in this big bothy all by myself. My day had been quite easy and I was up for a bit of revelry. Despite the fire, I couldn't get a decent heat in the room and I was still hungry after dinner. I had enough food to see me through the next couple of days, but no more. It was all a bit depressing and I went upstairs to my wooden floor early.

The gathering planned at Murlaggan took place in this area in May 1746 whilst Charles was in the Western Isles. This was the last Jacobite muster of the campaign. The chief's aim was to have a body of men for mutual protection whilst the government troops roamed the Highlands. But the numbers turned out were disappointing and with Charles gone the spirit was not there for further resistance. At the approach of a government force the Jacobites disbanded.

The following morning I was away early into Glen Mallie (Glen of the bare summit), crossing the river at the new bridge further upstream from the site of the previous one, which had been washed away. The glen was remote and undisturbed with the remnants of a Caledonian Forest on the south side and healthier groupings of trees by the river.

Glen Maillie

Snow-capped mountains under a blue sky painted a perfect picture. Unfortunately the weather deteriorated as the morning wore on and I took some cover at a lean-to by ruined Glenmallie cottage, where I had a break and pulled on the waterproofs once more.

I had received a call from BBC Radio Scotland the previous day and I was to be interviewed on the Fred MacAulay show just before noon. The satellite phone quite often cut conversations short, so I needed to be as high up a mountain as possible to try to get some reception on my mobile phone.

The track by the river became an ever-narrowing footpath and I left it to climb up onto the ridge that ran along the south side of Loch Arkaig and up to Gulvain. Crossing the ridge would allow me entry to Gleann Camgharaidh.

The route I chose seemed to be another deer superhighway and possibly an old route for driving cattle and sheep. Cresting the ridge, I headed up the final slopes of Gulvain that had just emerged from the mist.

At around 700m, I managed to find a spot on the wide ridge with mobile phone reception. It was an exposed location but I hunkered down out of the wind as best as I could to await the interview.

By the time the interview began, my body was frozen and so was my brain. I was delighted that the radio show was interested to see how I got on with my journey. Despite some mickey taking of a hiker with brain freeze, the interview went well and I told them of a few of the high points of my walk. Fred told me about some of the events of the real world that had taken place in the last six weeks, most of which I was quite glad to have missed.

Heading back down to pick up my pack, I continued towards Gleann Camgharaidh with the giant cliffs of Corrie Screamhaich (Screaming Corrie) towering over me. I stuck by the river, the rocky ground around the bank offering easier going than the surrounding moorland. Scrambling down by a large waterfall and having passed the crags of Gulvain, I headed in a south-westerly direction, aiming to cross the Camgharaidh River further upstream where it would be easier to cross. Despite the worries, the river was a pussycat, made even easier by a rickety wooden bridge. Two logs with planks nailed across them provided a shaky pathway over the river some distance below.

Gleann Camgharaidh possibly meaning Glen of the Crooked Hide-out (from Clan Cameron archives – http://www.clan-cameron. org/cam-ref.html) is a remote, barren glen with a south-west to north-east alignment, where the sharp peak of Streap overlooks its head, away in the distance. I walked up to the ruin of Glencamgarry cottage, the only remaining building in the glen where the Prince met up once more with Dr Archibald and Cluny MacPherson. These two had left the cage on Ben Alder before Charles got news of the French ships arrival. They had come to the Loch Arkaig area to discuss the position of and possibly retrieve some of the gold buried thereabouts. When the Prince's small party arrived they provided food and drink to sustain them until Loch nan Uamh was reached.

This glen may be where some of the Louis d'or, landed in April 1746, was buried. Although some was distributed to Jacobite chiefs at Murlaggan, the majority of the money was hidden on the shores of Loch Arkaig.

Whilst here, Charles promised Cluny MacPherson that he would return when it was within his power. He made a big ask of Cluny to remain in Scotland and keep the embers of the Rising burning. Cluny was also entrusted to look after the gold and for eight years he skulked in the Highlands keeping the Princes cause alive before Charles summoned him to France in 1754.

The usage of the treasure caused a great deal of argument and counter argument between the Jacobites in later years and eventually it even caused a rift between Charles and Cluny, with Charles accusing his great supporter of embezzlement. There are surviving accounts of the expenditure of the treasure by both Cluny and Dr Archibald

Gleann Camgharaidh waterfall

Cameron. It seems likely to me that at least a small proportion remains undiscovered. Murlaggan lies on the other side of Loch Arkaig from this glen so it is possible that the treasure was buried in this glen away from prying eyes and ferried over to Murlaggan to pay the chiefs in May 1746. Charles took 3,000 Louis d'or back to France with him and it would make sense that he collected it on his visit to the glen at this time.

After lunch I climbed up to the ridge forming the northern wall of the glen. Reaching the top I had magnificent views over the end of Loch Arkaig and into Glen Pean and Dessary. This area here seemed to be the apex of my walk and I had it in view for the third time. From here I had undertaken great journeys to the west and to the north; finally I was heading south-west to Loch nan Uamh and home.

I thought back to my struggle in Glen Pean (Pennyland glen) on the first week of the walk and realised how much more comfortable I was in the hills now. On the second occasion, how happy I was to meet George at Glen Pean Bothy, the moral support was invaluable at quite a difficult time. Now, I was on the home straight and had almost fulfilled my goal of having an adventure in the Scottish Highlands. I had achieved the inner peace I sought from the fulfilment of a long held desire.

Charles also must have felt a great euphoria at his escape. Against all odds he had remained outwith the clutches of the vast array of forces intent on his capture, enabling him to carry out the next phase of his plan. On his return to France, he wasted no time in petitioning the King for military aid so that he could return to his spiritual homeland to try again whilst the Highlands were aflame with rebellious sentiment.

I had visited many of Charlie's locations and found much of the territory to be unspoiled, a better location for an escape to the hills there never was. I had followed in his footsteps as accurately as possible. Where he had guides, I had maps and W.B Blaikie. Where he walked I had walked. He had belief in his cause and a belief that his survival was divine. I had determination to complete the journey with a little bit of common sense and a large dose of good fortune playing their part.

I continued along the crest of the undulating ridge, trying to keep out of sight of the soldiers down at the head of Loch Arkaig. Reaching the summit of Leac na Carnaich (569m), in front of me in the distance was the gigantic V-shaped saddle between the Munros of Streap and Sgurr Thuilm, Bealach a Chaorainn. What a sight, what a thought. I was tired already. To reach it I would need to drop down into Glen Cuirnean and take a well-trodden path climbing up to the pass.

Glen Cuirnean

I descended the steep slopes diagonally crossing gullies and avoiding crags to reach the floor of the glen as near the pass as possible. Climbing slowly up to the bealach at 471m, I felt exceptionally tired. Not even the thought of another bothy at Corryhully could pull me upwards and I counted steps to keep myself going. This was my fall-back, absolutely shattered option, and this was the first time I had resorted to it during the whole trip.

I carried on straight over the top of the pass and momentum carried my weary body downwards to the River Finan where a new one-megawatt hydroelectricity scheme was being built. Across the water was Corryhully bothy, a single room stone cottage featuring electric lighting! There was even firewood. Just sitting by the fireside, occasionally writing some notes was the perfect end to a tough day. Alistair Gibson, the Estate Manager at Glenfinnan pulled up in a Land Rover and seeing a light on, popped in to check on the bothy. He stopped for a chat and was keen to hear about my walk. I asked him for details about the surrounding area including whether he knew anything about the unusual looking island on the lochan in the hills above Loch Beoraid. I had spotted this island whilst climbing the hills

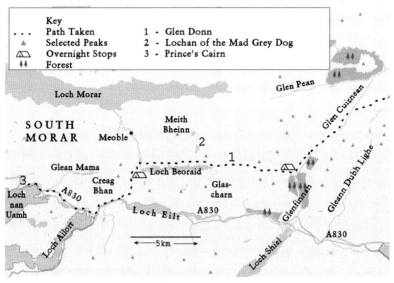

To Loch nan Uamh

to the south of Loch Beoraid on the day I left MacEachen's refuge some weeks before.

It transpired that in the early 19th century, a young MacDonald soldier returned from many years away to find that his beloved deerhound was still alive although it had left home and was living on this island. MacDonald set out to look for his dog and swam over to the island. The deerhound was absent but its four wild pups attacked him and tore him to pieces. Returning, the deerhound found its master dead and people from miles around heard its howls of despair. Afterwards, she hardly left MacDonald's side again, keeping watch by his graveside for the rest of her life.

Seeing my pitiful excuse for a fire, Alistair went up to the nearby lodge to bring back a pile of dry logs. Within no time I had a roasting blaze going. I sat up late and burned a stack of logs, enjoying the heat, and the atmosphere created. Meg lay on her blanket in front of the flames and didn't move an inch.

At midnight, as I was letting the fire die down, Meg started barking and just as my own hackles started to rise, the door opened and in from the black night came a hunched up, drenched, bedraggled hiker. I started the fire up once more and once he had got his wet clothes in front of the fire and consumed some hot food, he told me about his day.

Marco had recently graduated in Germany and was taking a walking holiday in Scotland before starting work as a physicist. He had left Bremen that morning and flown to Edinburgh. After taking in the sights of Edinburgh, he caught the last train to Mallaig. Getting off in the pitch dark at a deserted Glenfinnan Station he walked five kilometres along a forest path in the pouring rain here to the bothy. What a day! Starting off in the company of half a million busy Germans, here he was sharing a bothy at the head of a deserted glen, in remote countryside with one smelly Scot and his exhausted dug!

There were wooden benches on which to sleep and I lay long the next morning, listening to the rain as it drummed down on the metal roof. I was still ahead of schedule so I spent the morning in the bothy, reading old newspapers. A couple of ladies from Yorkshire came in to adjust their heavy packs. They were just starting the Cape Wrath Trail, a 320km walk from Fort William to Cape Wrath, the most north-westerly point on mainland Scotland. There is no set route for this trail but whatever route you take it's going to be a beautiful trek through remote territory. It looked to me like they were sporting too much weight on their backs, but I kept my mouth shut. I didn't want them ditching something on my say so, that they would later miss. We had a friendly chat whilst they patted Meg and I wished them all the best. My next guests were the local ramblers group who had walked up from Glenfinnan to see the hydroelectric scheme and came into the bothy to sit in a circle and eat their sandwiches.

At lunchtime, I made a start westwards once more, and followed the track into Caol Ghleann. The ATV track took me up this narrow chasm of a glen. Fraoch-bheinn was on my left, and I looked up at the precipitous slope that Charles was supposed to have descended and that I had backed out of earlier in my trip. I had made the right choice. I carried on along the glen, climbing steadily up to the bealach at 300m. The pass was littered with large dollops of glacier debris and was surrounded by untamed craggy slopes. With the mist providing a low ceiling there was a real land-that-time-forgot atmosphere. Yet another location virtually unchanged since the last ice age.

I looked down Glenn Donn towards Loch Beoraid. This descent

Corryhully Bothy with Caol Ghleann behind

had been worrying me, I had trouble with it before and that was during a dry weather spell. In the recent wet conditions it was going to be much worse. Alistair Gibson had told me of an old path higher up on the north side of the glen, partly falling away but possibly usable. Finding this old path I traversed the steep slopes of Meall Coire na Saobhaidh. It remained high while the glen fell away, and soon the river was 30m below. The path was narrow and exposed but only a couple of sections had disintegrated and it made exhilarating and fast work of a tough glen. As the valley finally levelled out near Loch Beoraid, the path descended down to the river, which I forded at the same place as previously, boots on as usual.

I passed the cottage at Kinlocharkaig, looking for a path along the north shores of Loch Beorad. Although this section of path is marked on the map Alistair had told me it was almost non-existent. In fact, it began underwater and I took to the adjacent hillside to begin my journey along the loch. Eventually the faint path emerged from the water and I followed it along the shoreline, where washed up driftwood cluttered the sandy sections of beach. The ins and outs of the barely visible path were slow going. The weather was dreich and my motivation was low. I was nearly at the end of the walk. Despite my lack of progress on this day, my fitness was at a lifetime high. Covering the miles was not a problem for my legs. My arms had had a good workout with the sticks and carrying the pack strengthened my upper body.

MacDonald of Lochgarry said of the Prince at this time that he had survived what few others could during his extended escape.

'Never was there a Highlander born could travel up and down hills better or suffer more fatigue.'

When questioned about handing Charles over for the huge reward Captain John MacKinnon of Elgol had said he 'wouldn't have done it for the whole world,' but he had also said that two of him could not have apprehended the Prince, as he was 'strong and nimble as anyone in the Highlands.'

Loch Beoraid is situated at the bottom of a deeply eroded valley, surrounded by high mountains and is graced with some tiny islands which the red deer swim out to feed on. The owners of Meoble estate have a wooden summerhouse that I could see on one of the islands hidden amongst the trees.

Loch Beoraid

On the summit plateau of the hillside above me was the Lochan of the Mad Grey Dog. The waterfall cascading down from the lochan was a wild delight and negotiating its torrents where they entered the loch, the trickiest yet that I had to cross. My feet were very nearly swept from under me.

At the end of a long afternoon, I reached the east end of the loch where the River Meoble carries away the water of Loch Beoraid to Loch Morar. A bridge over another hydroelectric scheme took me onto the steep hillside of Craig Bhan where the path headed south up to a pass and then descended down to Arieniskill.

MacEachen's refuge, my target once more, was just off the path and near the bealach but quickly the trail became vague and soon I lost it completely. I found myself scrambling up ridiculously steep slopes amongst trees and rocks. The vegetation camouflaged numerous fissures and cracks in the ground that could easily swallow a bounding Meg or an unwary leg. Using the cliffs above as a guide, I found a soaking wet MacEachen's refuge. Being open there were midge lodgers, the first time I had encountered any midges at all for the whole trip. I managed to eat my dinner in the cave and then I set up my tent on the soggy hillside, my final night under canvas where I reflected on what I could take from my trip.

I had hoped that being away from my everyday life would give me a better appreciation of what I had. By removing myself from the take-for-granted attitude of everyday living, I hoped to enjoy my home comforts all the more. I had missed my family of course and looked forward to spending time with them, catching up on the myriad things that must have happened since I had been away.

My self-confidence was high from having survived and prospered for the last six weeks and I enjoyed the feeling of being master of my own domain. I understood the power of setting a goal and working towards it. What I had only dared to dream 12 months previously had become a reality. No matter how impossible it had seemed at the time, I had achieved it. I must set more goals for the future and work towards them.

I had come to an understanding with Meg. I appreciated the help that she had been, the company she offered and how she looked after herself with hardly a word from me. The dog and I were bound in solid friendship.

The following day, I headed over the pass and descended towards Arieniskill where I had my first views of Lochailort, which makes up a part of the Sound of Arisaig. I had a late lunch in a little meadow by the Allt na Criche and made a list of the foods I never wanted to see again – cheese and onion risotto, banana custard, plain porridge and bags of unsalted catering nuts bought from a supermarket because they were cheap and full of goodness but almost inedible!

I joined the A830 and headed west, stopping at the Lochailort hotel for an Irn Bru. Somewhat appropriately, a picture on the wall of the homely bar was of Charlie's departure.

An evocative final text from Gary, an excerpt from the lyrics of *Wild Mountainside* by the Trashcan Sinatras:

'Beauty is within grasp, Hear the Highlands call, the last mile is upon us. I'll carry you if you fall.'

I continued on past a little church stunningly situated high on the hillside overlooking Loch Ailort, the interior of which was used in the filming of Local Hero. 'Our Lady of the Braes' was built to serve the people of the Ardnish Peninsula, a final poignant reminder of long vanished communities.

Finally, descending the road alongside Glen Mama, I saw Loch nan Uamh. Bloody hell. There it was, the end! The loch stretched away into the distance. A couple of fishing boats were anchored at its head. For Charles it was freedom as he saw the French ships *L'Heureux* and *Prince de Conti* in the bay.

The Prince left with some of his followers including Lochiel, Lochgarry and Doctor Cameron, outlawed men bereft of land and power. Among those left behind was John MacDonald of Borrodale who had shared in some of the Prince's most fraught and difficult adventures. Charles 'addressed himself to such as stayed behind to live in good hopes and that he expected to see us soon with such a force as would enable him to reimburse us for our losses and troubles so that he ended as he began.'

At 4am on 20 September, Charles sailed away under the cover of mist, in a scene that is reminiscent of the finale of *Lord of the Rings*. It wasn't the Undying Lands the Prince was going to but it may just as well have been, because although Charles lived a long time afterwards he was never to return. He 'left us all in a worse state than he found us,' said John MacDonald.

Loch nan Uamh

Two hundred and sixty six years later, the last attempts of the Stuarts to regain their rightful throne has become an immortal tale, where the ghosts of the heroes and villains can act out their parts for evermore on the unspoilt terrain of the Scottish Highlands and Islands. The rights and wrongs of the Rising will continue to be argued over but Charles gave everything that he had to avoid capture and continue the struggle after Culloden. His departure however, was the beginning of the end for the Highland clans. The very bonds that held them together would be torn asunder by the Act of Proscription as tartan, kilts, pipes and weapons were all banned. When the chiefs' rights of hereditary justice were also removed, they began to think of themselves not as leaders and protectors of the clan, but as landlords with estates to be maximised for monetary gain and not military produce.

My 800km walk was coming to an end, I had successfully recreated Charlie's journey and I was delighted with my success. I hurried on towards the cairn at Loch nan Uamh where Charles left Scotland forever. At the lay-by, my family were waiting. I strode on down the little track to the cairn and onto the slabs of rocks by the water's edge. I stepped into the water, raised my arms in celebration and turned round to meet my welcoming party. I hugged and kissed my family, tears flowing, and the Proclaimer's song '500 miles' playing in the background. What a welcome. Everyone talking at once. The noise level seemed incredible. Photos, smiles, togetherness. Most importantly to my youngest daughter Abbie, I had made it home in time for her birthday the following day.

For me the journey was the achievement of a lifetime. I had combined my love of Scotland's outdoors with the rich tapestry of its turbulent history. Despite the expected downpours, the unexpected snowstorms, the isolation of remote glens and towering mountains and my occasionally fragile mental state, the experience had been amazing. I had enjoyed it 100 per cent.

It was the achievement of a lifetime for the Prince as well. Never would his star shine as brightly as it did when he returned to France after what, for him, had been a heroic struggle, waged against the overwhelming government forces seeking to destroy him and the Highlanders who he had come to hold so dear.

Lochaber no More (1862) by J.B. Macdonald

Epilogue

CHARLES RETURNED TO France a hero for his brave attempt to win a crown for his father. The most talked about man in Europe, he wasted no time in gaining an audience with the King of France, Louis XV, to try and win support for an immediate landing of French troops in Scotland to relaunch his cause and help the ravaged Highlanders. When he failed to move the French, Charles tried unsuccessfully in Spain to find support.

Despite further intrigues and plots, no Jacobite campaign was ever launched against the House of Hanover again and Charles never did return to Scotland. With shifting European alliances, Charles became something of an embarrassment and then a downright problem firstly to France and then to the Pope himself. Charles' greatest days were behind him, moving around Europe, he became increasingly dependent on alcohol and eventually eroded much of the respect gained for his exploits of 1745–6. Charles died in 1788 without producing an heir and the succession passed to his brother Henry Cardinal Duke of York who died also without heir in 1807.

My own experience will, I hope, be somewhat different. On returning home I slipped quite seamlessly back into everyday life, due at least in part that I was reliving my adventure over and over again as I hammered away on the keyboard. As the writing has come to a close, I feel drawn back to the Highlands and Islands once again.

I look back with relish on glorious days outdoors, making my way through stunning scenery, enjoying unbounded freedom. Despite my relative lack of experience I had thrived outdoors and gained confidence in my own abilities whilst banishing some of my insecurities.

Charles' Rising and subsequent escape is now very much part of the history of the north-west Highlands and Islands but some of the marvellous journeys that he undertook deserve to be better known. The amazing combination of the history, the unspoiled terrain and the identifiable landmarks is completely enchanting to me; The dreams of a Jacobite victory yet remain at places like the cave at Elgol in Skye. Years after Charles had left, the McKinnon chief would return to the hollowed out cavern and sit and think through plans for a Stuart restoration before returning home much pleased with himself. Touching history as I had done and engaging with Charles by following in his footsteps during his escape was a privilege. Whilst I admire the physical and mental trials that Charles endured to in order to avoid capture I realise of course that these efforts were as nothing in comparison to the dreadful suffering of Highland communities in the aftermath of the Rising

For me the fulfilment of a long held goal, that for many years I had thought only to be a pipe dream, has been a tremendously satisfying achievement, but unlike Charles I will return – time and time again.

Timeline

Date	1746	Charles' Route – Day by Day	My timeline	2012
April	16	Battle of Culloden on Drummossie Moor	April	5
	17	Invergarry Castle, by Loch Oich in the Great Glen		7
	18	Glen Pean at the head of Loch Arkaig		8
	19	Between Oban and Meoble, South Morar		9
	20–26	Borrodale, Arisaig		10
	27–29	Rosinish peninsula, Isle of Benbecula, Western Isles		
	30 – 3 May	Isle of Scalpay, off Harris, Western Isles		12
May	4	Head of Loch Seaforth, Harris		12
	5	Kildun House, near Stornoway, Lewis, Western Isles		13
	6–9	Isle of Iubhard, off Lewis		
	10	Scalpay		
	11–13	Loch Uskavagh, Benbecula		14
	14–5 June	Glen Corradale, South Uist, Western Isles		16
June	6–9	Isle of Wiay, off Benbecula		14
	10–12	Rosinish peninsula, Benbecula		
	13–14	South Uist		14
	15–20	Loch Boisdale, South Uist		14
	20	Kenneths Hill, South Uist		14
	21	Ormiclate, South Uist		15
	21–22	Hecla, South Uist		16
	23	Isle of Wiay, off Benbecula		17
	24–27	Rosinish peninsula, Benbecula		18
	28	Prince's point, Trotternish Peninsula, Isle of Skye		19
	29	Kingsburgh, Isle of Skye		20

Date	1746	Charles' Route – Day by Day	My timeline	2012
June	30	Portree, Isle of Skye	April	20
July	1–2	Glam, Isle of Raasay		21
	3	North side of Portree Harbour		
	4	Elgol, Strathaird Peninsula, Isle of Skye		23
	5–7	Back on the mainland at Mallaig, North Morar.		23
	8	Eilean na Glaschoille off the Knoydart peninsula		24
	8	Morar, by Loch Morar		24
	9–12	Borrodale, Arisaig		25
	13–16	Macleods' Cove, Glen Mama, South Morar		25
	17	MacEachen's Refuge, South Morar		25
	18	Coire Odhar Mor, south-west of Sgurr nan Coireachan, near Glen Pean		27
	19	Meall an Fir- Oin, a northeasterly spur of Sgurr Thuilm overlooking the head of Loch Arkaig		27
	20	Summit of Drum Chosaidh in the Barrisdale Hills, west of Loch Quoich at the head of Glen Garry		28
	21	Coire Sgoiredail at the head of Loch Hourn		29
	22	Glen Shiel		29
	23	Hillside overlooking Loch Cluanie		30
	24–31	Coire Mheadoin, below Sail Chaorainn and north of Loch Cluanie.	May	2
August	1	Glen Affric		3
	2–4	Fasnakyle, Invernessshire, between Glen Affric and Glen Cannich		3
	5–8	Glen Cannich, Invernessshire		4
	9–11	Fasnakyle		4
	12–13	Glen Moriston		5
	14	Glen Garry		6
	15	Achnasaul near the foot of Loch Arkaig		7
	16–20	By Loch Arkaig		7
	21–22	Torr a Mhuilt, overlooking Achnacarry		7

Date	1746	Charles' Route – Day by Day	My timeline	2012
August	23–25	Meall a Tagraidh at the head of Glen Cia-Aig	May	6
	26–27	Achnacarry between Loch Arkaig and och Lochy		7
	28	Near Fort Augustus, south of Loch Ness in the Great Glen		9
	29	Coire an Lubhair Mor, north-east of Geal Charn in the Ardverikie hills, Badenoch		11
	30–1 Sept	By Loch Pattack between Loch Laggan and Loch Ericht, Badenoch.		11
September	2–4	By Allt a Chaoil-reidhe, between Loch Pattack and Ben Alder		11
	5–12	Southerly Slopes of Ben Alder, Badenoch		12
	13	By Allt a Chaoil-reidhe, between Loch Pattack and Ben Alder		12
	14	By Uisge nam Fichead in the Braeroy hills east of Glen Roy and north of Glen Spean.		14
	15	Between Glen Roy and the Great Glen		15
	16	Achnacarry		15
	17	Glen Camgaraidh, south of Loch Arkaig		16
	18	Heading towards the coast		17
	19	Borrodale, Arisaig.		18
	20	Boarded ship and departed for France		

Bibliography

Blaikie, W; *Itinerary of Prince Charles Edward Stuart*; Scottish History Society; Edinburgh; 1897.

Brown, H; *Hamish's Mountain Walk*; Sandstone Press; Dingwall; 2010.

Cawthorne, M; *Hell of a Journey*; Mercat Press; Edinburgh; 2004.

Clan Cameron Reference Guide, www.clan-cameron.org/cam-ref.html; 1995.

Death of William MacRae; www.northern.police.uk, home> Freedom of Information> Questions & Answers> operational.

Donaldson, W; *The Jacobite Song*; Aberdeen University Press; Aberdeen; 1988.

Duffy, C; *The '45*; Cassell; London; 2003.

Forbes, R; *The Lyon in Mourning*, 3 vols; Scottish History Society; Edinburgh; 1895.

Halldane, A; The Drove Roads of Scotland; Birlinn Edinburgh; 1997.

Home, J; *History of the Rebellion in Scotland in 1745*; Brown; Edinburgh; 1822.

Johnson, S & Boswell, J; *A Journey to the Western Islands of Scotland and The Journal of a Tour to the Hebrides*; Penguin; London; 1984.

Keys, D; *Mummification in Bronze Age Britain*; ww.bbc.co.uk/history/ancient/archaeology; 2011.

Lenman, B; *The Jacobite Cause*; Richard Drew Publishing; Glasgow; 1986.

Linklater, E; *The Prince in the Heather*; Granada; London; 1982.

Lord, S; *Walking with Charlie*; Pookus Publications; Witney; 2004.

MacCulloch, D; *Romantic Lochaber, Arisaig and Morar*; Chambers; Edinburgh; 1971.

MacDonald, C; *Moidart Among the Clanranalds*; Birlinn Limited; Edinburgh; 1997.

MacDonald, F; *Cocoa and Crabs, A Hebridean Childhood*; The Islands Book Trust; Isle of Lewis; 2009.

MacDonald, M; *The French MacDonald*; The Islands Book Trust; Isle of Lewis; 2007.

MacGregor, J; *In the Footsteps of Bonnie Prince Charlie*; BBC Books; London; 1998.

Mackenzie, W; *Simon Fraser, Lord Lovat: His Life and Times*; Chapman & Hall; London; 1908.

Maclean, F; *Bonnie Prince Charlie*; Weidenfeld and Nicholson; London; 1988.

McLynn, F; *Bonnie Prince Charlie*; Pimlico; London; 2003.

Murray, W ; *The Companion Guide to the West Highlands of Scotland*; Collins; London; 1969.

Nicholas, D; *The Young Adventurer*; The Batchworth Press; London; 1949.

Norie, W; *The Life and Adventures of Prince Charles Edward Stuart*, 4 vols; Caxton; London; 1903.

Oliver, N; *A History of Scotland*; Phoenix; London; 2010.

Pininski, P; *Bonnie Prince Charlie*; Ambereley Publishing; Stroud; 2010.

Pittock, M; *Jacobitism*; MacMillan Press Ltd; Hampshire; 1998.

Prebble, J; *Culloden*; Pimlico; London; 2002.

Prebble, J; *The Highland Clearances*; The Penguin Group; London; 1963.

Robertson, A; *Old Tracks Cross-country Routes and Coffin Roads in the North-west Highlands*; The Darien Press; Edinburgh; 1945.

Ross, D; *On the trail of Bonnie Prince Charlie*; Luath Press; Edinburgh; 2004.

Scottish Mountaineering Trust; *Hostile Habitats*; Scottish Mountaineering Trust; 2006.

Steel, T; *The Life and Death of St Kilda*; HarperCollins Publishers; London; 1994.

Tranter, N; *Gold for Prince Charlie*; Hodder and Stoughton; London; 1962.

Ure, J; *A Bird on the Wing*; Constable; London; 1992.

Wilkinson, C; *Bonnie Prince Charlie*; George G. Harrap & Co; London; 1932.

Some other books published by **LUATH** PRESS

Tales of Bonnie Prince Charlie and the Jacobites

Stuart McHardy
ISBN: 978-1-908373-23-6 £7.99 PBK

Great battles, great characters and great stories underpin our understanding of the Jacobite period; one of the most romanticised eras in Scottish history.

From the exploits of charismatic Bonnie Prince Charlie to the many ingenious ways the Jacobites outwitted the Redcoats, Stuart McHardy has gathered together some of the best tales from the period.

Find out the best way to escape from Edinburgh Castle and where to look for Prince Charlie's enchanted gold. Discover the story behind one Highlander who swapped his kilt for a dress, and more, in this salute to the ancient Scots tradition of storytelling.

On the Trail of Bonnie Prince Charlie

David R Ross
ISBN: 978-0-946487-68-5 £7.99 PBK

On the Trail of Bonnie Prince Charlie is the story of the Young Pretender. Born in Italy, grandson of James VII, at a time when the German house of Hanover was on the throne, his father was regarded by many as the rightful king. Bonnie Prince Charlie's campaign to retake the throne in his father's name changed the fate of Scotland. The Jacobite movement was responsible for the '45 Uprising, one of the most decisive times in Scottish history. The suffering following the battle of Culloden in 1746 still evokes emotion. Charles' own journey immediately after Culloden is well known: hiding in the heather, escaping to Skye with Flora MacDonald. Little is known of his return to London in 1750 incognito, where he converted to Protestantism (he reconverted to Catholicism before he died and is buried in the Vatican). He was often unwelcome in Europe after the failure of the uprising and came to hate any mention of Scotland and his lost chance.

Details of these and other books published by Luath Press can be found at:

www.luath.co.uk

Luath Press Limited

committed to publishing well written books worth reading

LUATH PRESS takes its name from Robert Burns, whose little collie Luath (*Gael.,* swift or nimble) tripped up Jean Armour at a wedding and gave him the chance to speak to the woman who was to be his wife and the abiding love of his life. Burns called one of 'The Twa Dogs' Luath after Cuchullin's hunting dog in Ossian's *Fingal*. Luath Press was established in 1981 in the heart of Burns country, and now resides a few steps up the road from Burns' first lodgings on Edinburgh's Royal Mile.

Luath offers you distinctive writing with a hint of unexpected pleasures.

Most bookshops in the UK, the US, Canada, Australia, New Zealand and parts of Europe either carry our books in stock or can order them for you. To order direct from us, please send a £sterling cheque, postal order, international money order or your credit card details (number, address of cardholder and expiry date) to us at the address below. Please add post and packing as follows: UK – £1.00 per delivery address; overseas surface mail – £2.50 per delivery address; overseas airmail – £3.50 for the first book to each delivery address, plus £1.00 for each additional book by airmail to the same address. If your order is a gift, we will happily enclose your card or message at no extra charge.

Luath Press Limited
543/2 Castlehill
The Royal Mile
Edinburgh EH1 2ND
Scotland
Telephone: 0131 225 4326 (24 hours)
Fax: 0131 225 4324
email: sales@luath.co.uk
Website: www.luath.co.uk